Date: 10/9/13

641.3 KUS
Kushner, Kim.
The modern menu : simple,
beautiful, kosher /

D1530628

PALM BEACH COUNTY
LIBRARY SYSTEM
3650 Summit Boulevard
West Palm Beach, FL 33406-4198

The M
Me

odern
nu

Simple
Beautiful
Kosher

Kim Kushner

Photography by Andrew Zuckerman
Introduction Photography by Nick Lee
Food styling by Victoria Granof

gefen
publishing house בית הוצאה לאור Est. 1981
JERUSALEM ◆ NEW YORK

Copyright © Kim Kushner Cuisine LLC
Jerusalem 2013/5773

All rights reserved. No part of this publication may
be translated, reproduced, stored in a retrieval
system or transmitted, in any form or by any means,
electronic, mechanical, photocopying, recording or
otherwise, without express written permission from
the publishers.

Book Design: Manual

Hardcover ISBN: 978-965-229-611-5
Softcover ISBN: 978-965-229-632-0

1 3 5 7 9 8 6 4 2

Gefen Publishing House Ltd.
6 Hatzvi Street
Jerusalem 94386, Israel
972-2-538-0247
orders@gefenpublishing.com

Gefen Books
11 Edison Place
Springfield, NJ 07081
516-593-1234
orders@gefenpublishing.com

www.gefenpublishing.com

Printed in Israel

Library of Congress Cataloging-in-Publication Data

Kushner, Kim.
  The modern menu : simple, beautiful, kosher / Kim
Kushner ; photography by Andrew Zuckerman ;
introduction photography by Nick Lee.
     pages cm
  Includes index.
  ISBN 978-965-229-611-5
1. Kosher food. 2. Comfort food. I. Title.
  TX724.K87 2013
  641.3--dc23
                        2012051186

For Jon

To my mind, less is more, simple is always best, and food should look as good as it tastes and taste as good as it looks.

A thoughtfully prepared dish is far more interesting than a perfectly prepared one. In fact, I never approach any dish with the idea that it will be perfect.

Introduction

The concept for this book has been building for the last decade. During these years I have been teaching, out of my own kitchen, various groups of friends how to cook and put together menus. As with most things in my life, this role as teacher happened somewhat serendipitously, when a friend who had sat at my table many times asked if I would give her and a few girlfriends some cooking tips. I agreed, and fell in love with teaching the moment I demonstrated the proper way to chop an onion. And I've been teaching ever since. There's nothing better than helping a fearful neophyte become a fearless cook, or turning a reluctant taster into a gourmand, or transforming a non-baker into a pastry pro. Not only is it gratifying to show students how to turn out simple, beautiful dinners, but it is even more satisfying to know that I had empowered them to take chances in the kitchen.

Before too long, I was receiving specific requests from my students. One wanted to prepare a meal that would reinvigorate her relationship with her husband. Another wanted to put her mother-in-law's pot roast to shame. The desires ran the gamut, but they all had one thing in common: my students wanted to use cooking as a way to make themselves and their families feel good. Cooking has always been my form of therapy and I was thrilled to help others use it as a tool to better their own lives.

Introduction

I have students who diligently take notes and faithfully reproduce every recipe to the letter. Some students need just a little guidance to set them on their way to cooking more varied and exciting dishes. Others come simply for the fun and camaraderie of cooking with like-minded women. But all leave with the important reminder that gathering around food is one of life's greatest pleasures. Indeed, I learned this from a very young age: I grew up in a food-loving family helmed by a mother who expressed all of her hopes and dreams through her food. Looking back, I now realize why my first instinct, whenever there's something to celebrate or commemorate, is to cook. When a friend has a baby, I bake a delicious cake. When new neighbors move into the building, I drop off a box of homemade biscotti. And whenever I feel the need to butter up my sons' teachers, I bake up a batch of sticky cinnamon rolls to share with them.

At the end of the day, everyone needs—and loves—to eat, especially when what's on offer is made with love. And the truth is, a thoughtfully prepared dish is far more interesting than a perfectly prepared one. In fact, I never approach any dish with the idea that it will be perfect. Not only is this attitude freeing, but it inspires me to try new ingredients, flavors, and techniques. To my mind, less is more, simple is always best, and food should look as good as it tastes and taste as good as it looks.

I've prepared the recipes in the following pages dozens of times; they're tried and true, foolproof, and beautiful. To a person, my students always want to know what goes with what, so I've organized the recipes into menus, named for the way the dishes make me feel. There's a Vibrant menu, filled with color, which inherently translates to flavor; the Crisp menu is loaded with pleasing crunch; the Saucy menu highlights the transformational power of a well-made yet simple sauce. The menu arrangements are simply suggestions; feel free to mix and match as you like. But never, ever skimp on the passion you put into making any dish, right down to a simple salad dressing. Because when it comes to cooking, what you put into it is what you get out of it.

Kim Kushner
New York City, 2013

Balsamic-Marinated Chicken with Olives and Sun-Dried Tomatoes — Page 85

Such strong childhood memories filter into everything that I make. It's never been about achieving perfection in the kitchen, only about achieving satisfaction—and a little bit of happiness. In my life, food is and always has been about sharing.

Food should taste as good as it looks, and look as good as it tastes. That's long been my abiding principle in the kitchen. I'm especially drawn to dishes that radiate bold, rich colors: the striking green of a freshly made pesto, the snow white interior of a slice of kohlrabi, the brick red of a bracing harissa.

I think about color as much as flavor and texture when I am composing a dish and a menu and always keep in mind that a delicious dish can never be too beautiful to eat. Dig in and enjoy your work of art.

Vibrant

Yes, I grew up eating kohlrabi, also known as a German turnip. It tastes like a mild version of broccoli and has the texture of an apple. I suppose it was part of my childhood diet because it is available year-round— at the grocery store, even. While my mother prepared it simply—sliced and drizzled with lemon juice—I prefer a slightly more interesting take, paired with cabbage and tossed in a delicious sweet-tart dressing.

4   bulbs kohlrabi
3   cups shredded green cabbage
⅓   cup dried cherries
¼   cup salted roasted sunflower seeds
¼   cup coarsely chopped fresh dill
¼   cup extra virgin olive oil
3   tablespoons pure maple syrup
    Zest of 1 lemon
    Juice of 2 lemons
1   garlic clove, minced
¼   teaspoon kosher salt
¼   teaspoon freshly ground black pepper

Using a sharp knife, remove the long stems and greens from the kohlrabi. Using a peeler, trim away the thick green skin until you reach the light green to white part that is free of tough fibers. Shred on the medium holes of a box grater or in a food processor fitted with the shredder disk.

Combine the kohlrabi, cabbage, cherries, sunflower seeds, and dill in a large serving bowl. In a small jar with a tight-fitting lid, combine the olive oil, maple syrup, lemon zest, lemon juice, garlic, salt, and pepper. Shake to thoroughly combine. Pour the dressing over the salad and toss to coat well. Let sit for about 20 minutes before serving.

Serves 6 to 8

Eggplant with Spicy Harissa Dipping Sauce

These slices are crispiest the day they are made, but I love them up to 2 days later! The harissa sauce will keep, refrigerated, up to a week. Harissa is a Tunisian hot chile sauce typically used in meat and fish stews as well as to flavor couscous. I serve these crispy eggplant slices as hors d'oeuvres or as a first course.

1   cup dried bread crumbs
2   teaspoons finely chopped fresh flat-leaf parsley, or other herb of your choice
½   teaspoon kosher salt
¼   teaspoon freshly ground black pepper
1   large eggplant, halved lengthwise and sliced into ¼-inch-thick slices
2   eggs, beaten
½   cup vegetable oil

Harissa Dipping Sauce
1   tablespoon harissa
    Juice of ½ lemon
1   tablespoon minced cilantro

Combine the bread crumbs, parsley, salt, and pepper in a medium bowl. Dip the eggplant slices into the beaten eggs, then roll around in the bread crumbs. Shake off excess and place on a baking sheet.

Heat ¼ cup of the oil in a large frying pan over medium-high heat. Working in batches, fry the eggplant until golden, about 30 seconds per side. Add the remaining oil as necessary to fry all the eggplant. As they cook, transfer the slices to a paper towel–lined plate to drain.

To make the harissa dipping sauce: Combine the harissa, lemon juice, and cilantro in a small bowl. Stir until thoroughly combined. Serve alongside the eggplant for dipping.

Serves 10

This recipe calls for frenched lamb chops, which are chops with the meat cut away from the end of the rib so that part of the bone is exposed. Frenching the chop makes it cleaner and let's call it fancier, almost like a lamb lollipop, if you will! Your butcher can do this with the quick swipe of a knife; asking him or her to do this makes fast work of this simple-to-prepare dish. Croute simply means "crust" in French. Fancy.

1   handful fresh basil, washed and dried well
½   handful cilantro, washed and dried well
3   garlic cloves, peeled
¼   cup extra virgin olive oil, plus more for drizzling
½   cup pine nuts, toasted
¼   cup unseasoned dried bread crumbs,
      plus more for sprinkling
      Kosher salt and freshly ground black pepper
12   baby lamb chops, frenched

Preheat the oven to 400°F.

In a food processor, combine the basil, cilantro, and garlic. Pulse until coarsely chopped. Add the olive oil and pine nuts and process until the mixture forms a paste, about 30 seconds. Transfer the mixture to a bowl, stir in the bread crumbs, and season with salt and pepper.

Season both sides of the lamb chops with salt and pepper. Prepare a grill or set a grill pan over high heat. Sear the lamb chops on both sides, about 1 minute per side. Transfer to a baking sheet.

Place a spoonful of pesto in the center of each chop, then spread it evenly over the surface. Sprinkle with additional bread crumbs and drizzle with olive oil. Bake until the crust is golden and crisp and the lamb is pink inside, about 10 minutes. Serve warm.

Serves 6

Couscous with Dried Fruit and Almonds

This dish not only presents beautifully and dramatically, but it fills the kitchen with such an intense fragrance that guests can't help but turn all of their attention to it. Whenever I serve this meatless side dish, it becomes the centerpiece of the meal; the colors are as vibrant as the flavor. Prepare the fruits and almonds ahead, if you like, and freeze until ready to use.

Couscous

1½	cups couscous
1	tablespoon margarine
1½	cups boiling chicken or vegetable stock or water
	Kosher salt and freshly ground pepper
1	tablespoon sugar
½	teaspoon cinnamon

Fruits and Almonds

2	tablespoons olive oil
3	medium onions, thinly sliced
¼	cup golden raisins
¼	cup dark raisins
¼	cup dried apricots
¼	cup almond slivers, lightly toasted
½	cup honey
1	teaspoon cinnamon, plus more for sprinkling
	Sugar, for sprinkling

To prepare the couscous: Pour the couscous into a large bowl. Stir the margarine into the boiling stock or water until melted. Pour over the couscous, cover with plastic wrap, and set aside for 15 minutes. Fluff the couscous with a fork, season with salt and pepper to taste, and sprinkle with the sugar and cinnamon.

Meanwhile, prepare the fruits and almonds: Heat the olive oil in a large sauté pan over medium-high heat. Add the onions and sauté until golden, about 10 minutes. Meanwhile, place the raisins in a small bowl, cover with boiling water, and let soak for 5 minutes. Drain well. Add the raisins, apricots, and almonds to the onions, stirring to combine. Pour the honey over the mixture along with ¼ cup water and the cinnamon. Cook, stirring, until all of the liquid is absorbed and the fruit sticks together, about 10 minutes.

Scoop the couscous into the center of a round, rimmed serving dish, forming a "mountain." Place the fruit mixture around the base of the couscous mountain and sprinkle additional cinnamon and sugar over the couscous.

Serves 6

Pomegranate seeds, lemon grass, lemons—this chapter is bursting with fresh, bright flavors that come from simple ingredients. When you use assertive ingredients, there's no need to use fussy techniques or complicated cooking methods to prepare delicious food. The recipes in this chapter exemplify my approach to cooking: the simpler the better. And the fresher the ingredients, the less you have to do to them to bring out their finest qualities.

To my mind, fresh food is clean food; it leaves you feeling satisfied not stuffed, nourished not nauseous. Broccoli is simply dressed and tossed with corn and red onion; halibut is brushed with a combination of lemongrass, ginger, chile, and garlic and simply baked; and cauliflower is tossed in tahini studded with glistening pomegranate seeds. In each of these dishes, the flavors are distinct and distinctly fresh.

Fresh

Sweet and Sour Broccoli Salad

The dressing to this salad is one I like to keep in my fridge. It works well with all salads, though I must say that the sweet and sour flavors work particularly well with broccoli.

1   head of broccoli, cut into tiny florets,
     stems peeled and cut into ¼-inch-thick pieces
1   (11-ounce) can corn niblets, drained
⅓   cup dried cherries or cranberries
3   tablespoons minced red onion
⅓   cup extra virgin olive oil
⅓   cup white vinegar
⅓   cup sugar
     Zest of 1 lemon

Combine the broccoli, corn, cherries, and red onion in a large bowl. Combine the olive oil, white vinegar, sugar, and lemon zest in a jar with a tight-fitting lid. Shake thoroughly to combine. Pour half of the dressing over the salad, toss well, and refrigerate for up to 30 minutes before serving. The remaining dressing will keep, refrigerated, up to 1 month.

Serves 6 to 8

Lemongrass Halibut with Cilantro and Peanuts

It's probably not every day that you pick up a stalk of lemongrass at the supermarket. I usually like sticking to ingredients that I am familiar with, but I recently took the plunge with lemongrass, and I am so glad that I did. Its bright flavor brings an exotic note to halibut. To use it, cut off the lower bulb and remove the tough, outer leaves.

6   (8-ounce) halibut fillets
1   stem lemongrass, chopped into 5 pieces
1   (3-inch) piece fresh ginger, peeled
2   garlic cloves, peeled
1   jalapeño pepper, stemmed and seeded
2   tablespoons soy sauce
1   teaspoon toasted sesame oil
1   teaspoon turmeric
½   teaspoon kosher salt
3   tablespoons chopped cilantro
3   tablespoons chopped salted roasted peanuts

Preheat the oven to 375°F. Line a baking sheet with parchment paper and place the fillets on the paper.

In a mini food processor, combine the lemongrass, ginger, garlic, jalapeño pepper, soy sauce, sesame oil, turmeric, and salt and process until chopped up and well combined. Brush the mixture over the fish fillets. Bake for 15 to 20 minutes, until the fillets are cooked through. Sprinkle the fillets with the cilantro and peanuts and serve.

Serves 6

Crunchy Curry Cauliflower with Tahini and Pomegranate

This is one of the best ways—actually, my favorite way—to prepare cauliflower. It is adapted from a wonderful recipe from the Ottolenghi cookbook. The cauliflower can be made in advance, refrigerated overnight, and reheated. The tahini dressing can be made up to a week in advance and refrigerated, though I like to bring it to room temperature before serving.

2	heads of cauliflower, cut into florets
¼	cup olive oil
2	tablespoons curry powder
½	cup pomegranate seeds

Tahini Dressing

¼	cup tahini paste
	Juice of ½ lemon
2	garlic cloves, minced
2	tablespoons minced cilantro
1½	teaspoons kosher salt
½	teaspoon freshly ground black pepper

Preheat the oven to 400°F. Combine the cauliflower, olive oil, and curry powder in a large bowl and toss to coat. Transfer to a baking dish, cover with foil, and bake for about 20 minutes, until the cauliflower is softened. Remove the foil and bake for 30 minutes longer, until golden and crisp. Transfer to a serving dish.

Meanwhile, prepare the tahini dressing: Combine the tahini paste, lemon juice, garlic, cilantro, salt, pepper, and ¼ cup water in a jar with a tight-fitting lid. Shake to thoroughly combine.

Drizzle a couple of spoonfuls of the dressing over the warm or cooled cauliflower and sprinkle the pomegranate seeds over.

The remaining dressing will keep, refrigerated, up to 2 weeks.

Serves 6 to 8

This pasta is wonderful served all year-round. Add grilled chicken or fish for an all-in-one meal. It's also amazing with grated Parmesan cheese or bocconcini.

16   **ounces farfalle pasta**
½   **cup cilantro leaves**
½   **cup fresh flat-leaf parsley leaves**
2   **garlic cloves, peeled**
½   **cup shelled pistachios**
⅓   **cup extra virgin olive oil**
½   **teaspoon kosher salt**
½   **teaspoon freshly ground black pepper**

Cook the pasta according to package directions. Drain and set aside.

Meanwhile, place the cilantro, parsley, and garlic in a food processor and process until finely chopped. Add the pistachios and olive oil and process until a paste is formed. Transfer to a large serving bowl and stir in the salt and pepper. Add the drained pasta to the pesto, toss to coat, and serve warm or at room temperature.

Serves 6 to 8

Is there anything more satisfying than the sound a bite into a cool radish makes? Or the crackling of a flaky, golden, puff-pastry crust? This menu features dishes that elicit those most pleasurable sounds. But when it comes to food, crisp is not only a sound and a texture, it's also a look.

The recipes that follow are fresh and striking—the kind of dishes that you first eat with your eyes. Each one features a crisp ingredient—crunchy panko crumbs, colorful cabbage shreds, fresh Kirby cucumbers—as part of the mix. There's nothing better to sink your teeth into.

Crisp

Radish, Fava Bean, and Edamame Salad

Short, fat Kirby cucumbers are ideal for this salad because the peel, which you leave on, isn't the least bit bitter, unlike the peel from Kirby's longer, skinnier counterparts. This is a lush, vividly colored salad, best made when cucumbers and radishes are at their peak.

The dressing and the salad can be prepared and refrigerated, separately, up to 1 day in advance. Add the dressing to the salad just before serving.

2   Kirby cucumbers, cut crosswise at an angle into ¼-inch-thick slices
1   cup thinly sliced radishes
1   cup frozen shelled fava beans, thawed
1   cup frozen shelled edamame, thawed
3   tablespoons white vinegar
1½ tablespoons extra virgin olive oil
2   teaspoons sugar
1   teaspoon toasted sesame oil
1   tablespoon black sesame seeds

Combine the cucumbers, radishes, fava beans, and edamame in a medium bowl. Cover and refrigerate. Combine the white vinegar, olive oil, sugar, sesame oil, and sesame seeds in a small bowl and whisk together. Pour over the salad, toss, and serve.

Serves 6

Crunchy Cabbage Salad

→ Image on page 52

I've made this simple-to-prepare salad dozens of times with impeccable results. It's great for lunch, brunch, or a casual dinner. Shred the cabbage by hand rather than running it through the food processor; I find it stays crunchier longer. An entire hand-shredded cabbage will keep, wrapped in paper towels in a resealable plastic bag, for up to 2 weeks. I double—or even triple—the dressing so that I have it on hand; it'll keep in the refrigerator for up to 1 month. It can also be used as a wonderful marinade for veggies, meats, and chicken.

¼ cup soy sauce
¼ cup white vinegar
¼ cup packed brown sugar
¼ cup extra virgin olive oil
1 small red cabbage, shredded on the large holes of a box grater, about 5 cups
  Seeds from 1 pomegranate
½ cup chopped salted cashews
½ cup chopped cilantro, plus a few sprigs for garnish
3 tablespoons poppy seeds

Combine the soy sauce, vinegar, brown sugar, and olive oil in a jar with a tight-fitting lid. Shake to thoroughly combine. (Makes 1 cup.)

In a large bowl, combine the cabbage, pomegranate seeds, cashews, cilantro, and poppy seeds. Pour half of the dressing over and toss to thoroughly coat, adding more if necessary. Garnish with the cilantro sprigs and serve.

Serves 6 to 8

Grilled Vegetables

→ Image on page 15

If you don't already own an indoor grill pan, run—don't walk—to the kitchen store and get one. A grill pan has a grooved surface that chars your food in the same way an outdoor grill does. I use it to sear all my steaks, chops, and chicken and lock in the flavor. But admittedly, I love the striking grill marks, too! The same goes for vegetables. Once I get a good sear, I complete the cooking in the oven.

1   bunch asparagus, woody stems trimmed
3   medium red onions, thickly sliced
2   red, green, or yellow bell peppers, cored and cut into large pieces
2   zucchini, sliced lengthwise into ¼-inch-thick strips
1   large eggplant, sliced lengthwise into ¼-inch-thick strips
2   cups white mushrooms
½   cup olive oil
1   teaspoon dried basil
1   teaspoon kosher salt
½   teaspoon freshly ground black pepper
    Zest and juice of 1 lemon
3   tablespoons good-quality balsamic vinegar

Place half of the asparagus, onions, peppers, zucchini, eggplant, and mushrooms in each of two large resealable plastic bags. In a small bowl, whisk together the olive oil, basil, salt, pepper, and lemon zest. Pour half into each of the bags and seal. Marinate, turning the bags over once or twice to evenly coat the vegetables, for at least 1 hour, or up to 24 hours in the refrigerator.

Preheat the oven to 400°F. Heat a grill pan over medium-high heat until it is too hot to hold your hand 3 inches above the grill for more than a few seconds. Using tongs and working in batches, remove the vegetables from the marinade and place on the grill pan in a single layer. Reserve the marinade. Grill each batch, turning the vegetables once, for 3 minutes on each side, until nice grill marks form.

Transfer the vegetables to 2 large baking sheets and arrange in a single layer. Pour the reserved marinade over the vegetables. Roast for about 10 minutes, until the vegetables are soft in the center and crunchy on the edges. Transfer to a serving platter. Drizzle with the lemon juice and balsamic vinegar. Serve warm or at room temperature.

Serves 6 to 8

I like to use paper baking molds for these pretty little tarts because they can be baked in the oven, and then easily peeled away for a beautiful presentation. They are readily available online—including from one of my favorite sources for baking supplies, GoldasKitchen.com.

¼   cup balsamic vinegar
1   tablespoon margarine or butter
1   tablespoon sugar
4   sweet onions, cut into thin rounds
1   sheet frozen puff pastry (½ of a 17-ounce package), thawed
      Fresh thyme leaves to garnish

Combine the vinegar, margarine, and sugar in a small saucepan and bring to a boil. Immediately remove from the heat and let cool. Place the onions in a large resealable bag and pour the vinegar mixture over them. Seal the bag and marinate the onions for at least 30 minutes, or up to 48 hours in the refrigerator.

Roll the puff pastry dough out to a ¼-inch-thick 10 x 15-inch rectangle. Using a 5-inch round cookie cutter, cut out 6 rounds of dough. Place on a baking sheet lined with parchment and prick all over with a fork. Cover and refrigerate for 20 minutes.

Preheat the oven to 425°F.

Remove the onions from the marinade and divide among six 3½-inch round tart molds. Place a round of puff pastry over each, and gently press down around the inside edges to cover the onions entirely. Place the molds on a baking sheet and bake for about 20 minutes, until golden brown. Immediately invert the tartlets onto a platter and carefully remove the molds. Garnish with the thyme and serve.

Makes six 3½-inch tarts

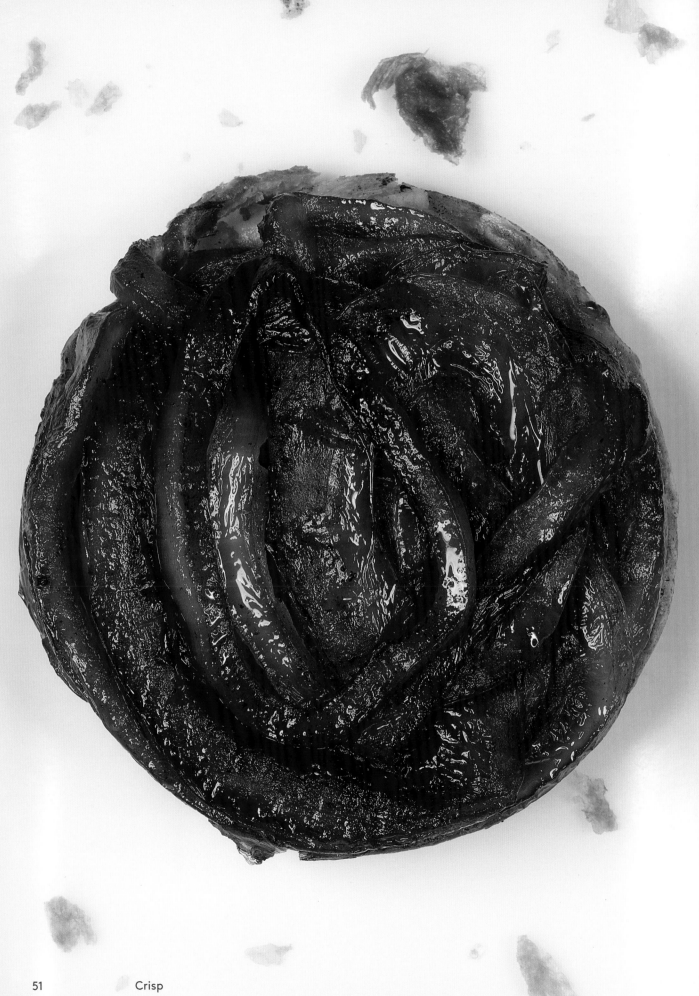

Here's a somewhat sophisticated version of the standard breaded cutlet, thanks to the use of Japanese ingredients—miso, ume plum vinegar, mirin, and panko crumbs. They're all readily available (and most in kosher options) at your local supermarket or health food store. They've become staples in my pantry; I use them in various combinations for dressings and sauces. You might say I'm hooked!

¼ cup packed light brown sugar
2 heaping tablespoons white miso paste
½ cup ume plum vinegar or rice vinegar
3 tablespoons mirin
2 teaspoons soy sauce
6 chicken cutlets
1-2 cups panko crumbs
¼ cup vegetable oil

In a medium bowl, whisk together the brown sugar, miso, vinegar, mirin, and soy sauce. Place the cutlets in a resealable plastic bag and pour half the marinade over them. Seal the bag and marinate the chicken for at least 30 minutes, or up to 12 hours in the refrigerator. Cover and refrigerate the remaining marinade.

Preheat the oven to 150°F. Arrange a few layers of paper towels on a large plate or platter. Place the panko crumbs on a large dinner plate. Heat the vegetable oil in a large frying pan over medium-high heat. Remove the cutlets from the marinade and dredge in the panko crumbs, coating both sides evenly. (Discard the chicken marinade and the plastic bag.) When the oil is hot but not smoking, slip 2 cutlets into the pan and cook until dark golden and crisp, about 2 to 3 minutes per side. Transfer to the paper towel–lined platter with a slotted spatula to drain. Repeat with the remaining cutlets.

Transfer the cutlets to a baking sheet to keep warm while the remaining batches are cooking. Drizzle the reserved marinade over the chicken just before serving, or serve in a bowl alongside the cutlets.

Serves 6

Everyone's idea of comfort foods is slightly different, but no matter the dish, they all have one thing in common: the power to take you back to a homey place with familiar aromas and beloved family and friends. Just one bite of a favorite comfort food is all it takes to summon the warm feelings of home, of family. But even before your mother's lasagna or grandmother's chicken soup or father's special pasta passes your lips, my guess is that the dish's fragrance is enough to take you back.

I grew up eating hearts of palm and corn salad; to this day, I equate the smell of dill with the kitchen of my childhood. My Aunt Esther's roast chicken has become my husband Jon's favorite meal. And my children are growing up eating my mother's cinnamon-scented potatoes. The foods of our childhood anchor us, keep us connected, and carry such strong, happy associations that they inspire us to pass them down to future generations. There's nothing more nourishing than that.

Nourishing

Red Cabbage and Beet Salad with Sesame-Soy Dressing

Simple and impressive—what else can I say? I like to use a food processor fitted with a shredding disk to grate the beets, but a box grater works just fine.

3   medium beets, peeled and grated
3   cups shredded red cabbage
½   cup sesame seeds
⅓   cup roughly chopped fresh dill
1½   tablespoons sugar
¼   cup extra virgin olive oil
     Juice of 2 limes
3   tablespoons soy sauce
½   teaspoon toasted sesame oil

Combine the beets, cabbage, sesame seeds, and dill in a large serving bowl. Combine the sugar, olive oil, lime juice, soy sauce, and sesame oil in a jar with a tight-fitting lid. Shake to thoroughly combine. Pour over the salad and toss to coat thoroughly.

Serves 6 to 8

Corn Salad with Fennel and Hearts of Palm

I like to arrange the large outer leaves of the endive around the rim of a round platter, like petals on a flower.

1   fennel bulb, trimmed of tough inedible parts and halved lengthwise
5   hearts of palm, cut into ¼-inch rounds
5   endives, large outer leaves removed and set aside for garnish
3   ears corn, kernels cut from cobs
⅓   cup extra virgin olive oil
¼   cup balsamic vinegar
1   tablespoon Dijon mustard
1   tablespoon sugar
½   teaspoon dried oregano

Lay each fennel half on a cutting board, flat side down, and cut crosswise into thin slices. Transfer to a large bowl or serving platter and add the hearts of palm. Slice each endive, beginning at the top of the head, crosswise into ¼-inch-thick slices. Add to the bowl followed by the corn kernels.

Combine the olive oil, vinegar, mustard, sugar, oregano, and 2 tablespoons of water in a jar with a tight-fitting lid. Shake to thoroughly combine. Mound the salad on a large serving plate and drizzle with the dressing. Garnish with the large endive leaves and serve immediately.

Serves 8

Jon's Roast Chicken

This dish, a weekly staple in my house and my husband Jon's favorite, is a perfect example of how a few top-quality ingredients are all you need to make a fabulous meal. Cooking this chicken on a vertical chicken roaster stand (available online) allows you to roast a whole chicken in an upright position. The result is unfailingly moist and juicy chicken. In a pinch, you can use an empty soda can! The chicken tastes best the day it is roasted.

1   (3-to 4-pound) roaster chicken
    Kosher salt and freshly ground black pepper
2   lemons, halved
1   garlic bulb
1   teaspoon olive oil
10 fresh thyme sprigs

Preheat the oven to 400°F. Rinse the chicken under cold running water and pat dry with paper towels. Generously season the chicken inside and out with salt and pepper. Squeeze the juice of 1 lemon into the chicken's cavity and then stuff what's left of it into the cavity. Squeeze the juice of the remaining lemon all over the outside of the chicken and throw the halves into the pan.

Cut a ¼-inch slice off the top of the garlic bulb and discard the top. The garlic cloves should be peeking out of the top. Place the bulb on a piece of aluminum foil, drizzle the oil over the top, and wrap tightly. Stuff the garlic into the chicken cavity followed by 4 thyme sprigs.

Insert the roaster stand into the chicken cavity, pushing it in as far as it will go. Stand the chicken in a roasting pan and place the remaining thyme sprigs over the chicken. Roast for 1 hour. Reduce the temperature to 325°F and roast for an additional 20 minutes, until cooked through to the bone and the juices run clear at the thickest part of the breast. Let cool slightly.

Carefully remove the lemon and wrapped garlic from the chicken cavity. Discard the thyme sprigs. Squeeze any juice from the cooked lemons over the chicken, then discard. Unwrap the garlic and squeeze the softened cloves over the chicken. Cut the chicken into eight pieces and serve warm. Alternatively, let it come to room temperature before serving.

Serves 4 to 6

This dish is great for those nights
when the side dish is an afterthought.
Chances are you'll have all of the
ingredients in your pantry, and if
you don't have sweet potatoes, you
can make it without them. My mom
always used to make these for my
siblings and me when we were young;
as soon as she pulled the pan from the
oven, we would go at the crispy bits
with our forks.

6   Yukon gold potatoes, scrubbed and
     cut into 6 to 8 wedges each
3   sweet potatoes, scrubbed and
     cut into 6 to 8 wedges each
¼   cup olive oil
2   tablespoons dried basil
1   teaspoon kosher salt
½   teaspoon cinnamon
½   teaspoon freshly ground black pepper

Preheat the oven to 350°F. In a large roasting pan,
combine the potatoes, sweet potatoes, olive oil, basil,
salt, cinnamon, and black pepper. Toss well.

Roast, uncovered, until the potatoes are soft on the
inside and crisp on the edges, about 2 hours. Roast
an additional 30 minutes if you prefer your potatoes
very crispy.

Serves 6 to 8

What is warm food? It's the kind of food I think about when I picture a small group of friends sitting around a fireplace. It's dishes that, whether through temperature or flavor or texture, can chase away a chill unlike any other. It may seem counterintuitive, but a salad of mixed greens topped with crispy croutons is warm food.

What could be better than the crunch of a crouton? Gingery crab cakes, too, are warm food, not least because of the power of ginger to soothe and heal. And is there anything more succulent and warm than chicken braised so slowly that it falls off the bone?

Crunchy Gingered "Crab" Croquettes

I've always wanted to try a crab cake, so I made them the kosher way, with surimi (mock crabmeat, usually made from white-fleshed fish like hake or pollock), fresh ginger, lime juice, and cilantro. Serve as an appetizer at a dinner party or as hors d'oeuvres. The recipe also uses my two all-time favorite pantry essentials: Spicy Mayo, and Spicy Crunchies—spiced and toasted rice cereal. They're worth having on hand whether you make these delicious crab cakes or not. I use them to top salads and dress pasta or grilled fish or chicken.

Spicy Crunchies

2	cups crisped rice cereal (such as Rice Krispies)
2	tablespoons olive oil
1	tablespoon cayenne pepper

Spicy Mayo

½	cup mayonnaise
1	tablespoon Tabasco sauce, or more to taste
1	teaspoon sugar
1	teaspoon sesame oil
½	teaspoon chili powder

Croquettes

1	(16-ounce) package surimi (imitation crabmeat), about 16 crabsticks
	Juice of 1½ limes
¼	cup fresh dill
¼	cup fresh cilantro
1	(3-inch) piece fresh ginger, peeled
3	eggs
2	tablespoons flour
1	teaspoon kosher salt
½	teaspoon freshly ground black pepper
½	cup vegetable oil

To make the Spicy Crunchies: Preheat the oven to 400°F. In a large bowl, combine the cereal, olive oil, and cayenne. Spread on a large baking sheet in a single layer. Bake for 10 minutes, until golden. Let cool completely. Using your hands, crush the crunchies to break them up a bit. Makes about 2 cups. Meanwhile, make the Spicy Mayo: Whisk together the mayonnaise, Tabasco, sugar, sesame oil, and chili powder until well combined. Add more Tabasco, if desired. Makes about ½ cup. The sauce will keep, tightly covered in the refrigerator, for up to 4 days.

To make the croquettes: Cut the crabsticks in half and place in a food processor. Add the lime juice, dill, cilantro, and ginger and process until fine and crumbly, about 2 minutes. Transfer to a large bowl. Add the eggs, ¼ cup of the Spicy Mayo, and 1 cup of the Spicy Crunchies, using your hands to combine. Stir in the flour, salt, and pepper. Cover and refrigerate for 30 minutes or up to 12 hours.

Preheat the oven to 400°F. Line a baking sheet with parchment. With damp hands, form about 20 golf ball–sized balls from the surimi mixture. Place on the baking sheet and flatten slightly with the palm of your hand, rewetting it as necessary.

Heat the oil in a large sauté pan over medium-high heat. In batches, add the croquettes and sauté until golden, about 2 minutes per side. Transfer to a paper towel–lined tray to drain, then return to the baking sheet. Bake for about 10 minutes, until plump and firm to touch. Serve with the remaining Spicy Mayo for dipping.

Makes about 20 croquettes

Every time I go out to dinner, I quickly scan the menu hoping to find a salad just like this one. It's what I refer to as a "big salad" because it's fresh and filling: crisp romaine lettuce, bright peppers, juicy tomatoes, crunchy "croutons" (actually pieces of spiced toasted tortillas). Sometimes it just doesn't get any better, especially if you eat it on a comfy couch under a cozy blanket. The croutons, seasoned with sumac (a tart, rich, red spice) can be made a few days in advance and stored in an airtight container or a resealable plastic bag.

Croutons
2	tablespoons olive oil
1	clove garlic, minced
1	teaspoon sumac
4	flour tortilla wraps of any kind

Tangy Dressing
¼	cup extra virgin olive oil
	Juice of 2 lemons
2	garlic cloves, minced
2	teaspoons sumac
¼	teaspoon kosher salt
¼	teaspoon freshly ground black pepper

Salad
2	heads romaine lettuce, finely chopped
1	red bell pepper, cored, seeded, and cut into medium dice
1	green bell pepper, cored, seeded, and cut into medium dice
1	large tomato, seeded and cut into medium dice
2	Kirby cucumbers, peel on, cut into medium dice
¼	cup minced fresh flat-leaf parsley
2	tablespoons minced onion
2	tablespoons minced fresh mint

To make the croutons: Preheat the oven to 375°F. In a small bowl, stir together the olive oil, garlic, and sumac. Place the tortillas on a baking sheet and brush the garlic mixture evenly over each. Bake until crisp, about 8 minutes, checking every few minutes to avoid burning. Let cool, then break into small pieces.

Meanwhile, make the dressing: Combine the olive oil, lemon juice, garlic, sumac, salt, and pepper in a jar with a tight-fitting lid. Shake to thoroughly combine. Alternatively, place all ingredients in a mini food processor and blend to combine. Makes about ½ cup. The dressing will keep, refrigerated, for up to 1 month.

To assemble the salad: Combine the lettuce, peppers, tomato, cucumbers, parsley, onion, and mint in a large serving bowl and toss. Top with the croutons, drizzle all of the dressing over, and serve.

Serves 8

Chicken with Pumpkin, Figs, and Honey

The ultimate in richness and flavor. This beautiful recipe is a staple at our holiday meals. It is a perfect example of elevating chicken to the next level. The combination of red wine, pumpkin, and figs, along with fresh herbs, really creates a magical dish. Proof that you don't need to serve expensive cuts of meat to make it impressive.

12 pieces skinless bone-in chicken, white or dark meat
    Kosher salt and freshly ground black pepper
2   onions, peeled
2   cloves garlic, peeled
    Leaves from 6 sprigs fresh thyme
    Needles from 2 sprigs fresh rosemary
3   tablespoons olive oil
1   (15-ounce) can plain pumpkin puree
1   cup red wine
¼   cup honey
1   cup dried Mission figlets or 2 cups fresh figs, stemmed
2   cinnamon sticks, cracked
1   teaspoon ground allspice
    Slivered almonds, toasted

Season the chicken pieces with salt and pepper and set aside. Combine the onions, garlic, thyme, and rosemary in the bowl of a food processor and pulse once or twice; do not allow the mixture to become mushy.

Heat the oil in a heavy skillet or Dutch oven over medium-high heat. Add the onion mixture and sauté until soft and fragrant, about 6 minutes. Push the onions to the side, add the chicken in batches, and brown for several minutes on all sides.

Meanwhile, in a large bowl, whisk together the pumpkin puree, wine, honey, figs, cinnamon, allspice, and 1¼ cups water. (This is usually the point where I pour myself a glass of red. Once the bottle is open, why not?) Pour over the chicken to cover. (The aroma is beyond at this point!) Bring to a boil, then reduce the heat to medium. Cover and cook until the chicken looks plump and is cooked through, and the aroma is too much for you to handle, 45 minutes for white meat and up to 1 hour for dark meat. Discard the cinnamon sticks. Place the chicken pieces on a serving platter, spoon the sauce over, and sprinkle the toasted almonds over the top.

Serves 8

Bourekas

Bourekas are small baked pastries made from filo dough or puff pastry dough and filled with savory fillings such as potatoes and cheese.

30   pre-cut 5-inch frozen puff pastry squares
      Boureka filling of your choice (see opposite)
1   egg, lightly beaten
      Sesame seeds

Line 2 baking sheets with parchment paper. Place the pastry squares on the baking sheets, spaced 1 inch apart. Set aside for several minutes, until the squares begin to thaw.

Place a heaping teaspoon of filling in the center of a square and fold over on the diagonal, forming a triangle. Gently press down on the corners to adhere. Repeat until all squares are filled. (The bourekas can be frozen at this point: Place the baking sheets in the freezer for several hours until the bourekas are completely frozen. Transfer them to resealable plastic bags and freeze for up to 6 months.)

Preheat the oven to 400°F. Brush the bourekas with the beaten egg and sprinkle with sesame seeds. Bake for 20 minutes, until golden brown and crispy. For frozen bourekas, place them on a baking sheet straight from the freezer and bake for 20 to 25 minutes.

Makes 30 bourekas

Long Boureka

This larger variation is great to make when you are short on time! Note that you'll need to use a thawed puff pastry sheet instead of the squares.

Preheat the oven to 400°F. Lay a sheet of puff pastry (½ of a 17-ounce package) on a parchment-lined baking sheet. Roll out to a ½-inch thickness. Spread on the filling, leaving a 2-inch border. With a long side of the pastry facing you, roll up the pastry (like a yoga mat!). Pinch together the edges to close them. Using a very sharp knife, make diagonal slashes on the top of the roll running the entire length of the pastry. Brush all over with beaten egg, sprinkle with sesame seeds, and bake for 25 to 30 minutes. Cut into 2-inch slices and serve warm.

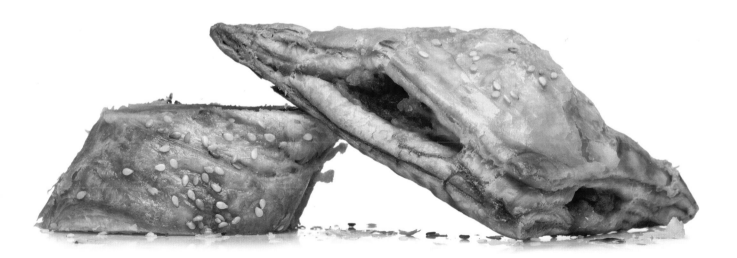

Caramelized Onions

There is nothing that enhances a recipe quite like sweet, rich caramelized onions, so I always have them on hand. My cooking students have raved over them and some have even said they've changed the way they cook.

Peel 2½ pounds onions, halve, and slice thinly into half rounds. Heat about 3 tablespoons olive oil in a large skillet over medium heat, add the onions, and cook, stirring occasionally, until they are completely softened and deeply browned, about 45 minutes. (When I have a lot of time, I slice tons of onions—sometimes 10 pounds!—and have 4 pans going on the stovetop at once.) Cool the sautéed onions completely and divide into 1-cup portions. Transfer to plastic freezer bags and freeze until needed.

Whenever you are cooking just about anything, take a bag out of the freezer and let it thaw on the counter (you may microwave it to defrost as well). Add to soups, stews, chicken, fish, rice dishes... any dish! They are perfect in ground beef when you make hamburgers, meatballs, and meatloaf, or stir them into white rice or grains to add some flavor and sophistication.

Sweet Potato, Pumpkin, and Pecan Filling

I add a drop of maple syrup to the beaten egg before brushing the bourekas filled with this fragrant fall mixture.

3   sweet potatoes, peeled
½   cup canned pumpkin puree
¼   cup toasted pecans, roughly chopped
½   teaspoon cinnamon
¼   teaspoon nutmeg
    Kosher salt and freshly ground pepper

Cook the potatoes in a large pot of salted boiling water for about 20 minutes, until just tender. Mash the potatoes using a masher or potato ricer. Stir in the pumpkin, pecans, cinnamon, and nutmeg. Season with salt and pepper. Let cool.

Ricotta and Spinach Filling

1   (10-ounce) package frozen chopped spinach, thawed and drained well
1   (15-ounce) container ricotta cheese
1   teaspoon garlic powder
    Dash nutmeg
    Kosher salt and freshly ground pepper

Combine the spinach, ricotta, garlic powder, and nutmeg and stir to combine. Season with salt and pepper.

Sautéed Vegetable Filling

Garlicky spinach, mushrooms, onions, and red peppers make up this delicious filling, best used only for the long boureka; it's a bit too loose for the individual pastries.

2   tablespoons olive oil
1   red bell pepper, cored and julienned
1   (10-ounce) package frozen chopped spinach, thawed and drained well
2   cups sliced mushrooms
¼   cup Caramelized Onions, page 69
1   clove garlic, minced
1   teaspoon lemon zest
    Kosher salt and freshly ground black pepper

Heat the oil in a large sauté pan over medium-high heat. Add the red pepper, spinach, mushrooms, and onions. Sauté until soft and fragrant, about 5 minutes. Add the garlic and lemon zest. Season generously with salt and pepper. Sauté for 5 minutes more. Let cool.

Potato and Caramelized Onion Filling

5   Yukon gold potatoes, peeled
½   cup Caramelized Onions, page 69
    Kosher salt and freshly ground black pepper

Cook the potatoes in a large pot of salted boiling water for about 20 minutes, until a fork is easily inserted into one. Drain and mash the potatoes using a hand masher or potato ricer. Stir in the onions and season generously with salt and pepper. Let cool.

There is no better word to describe the dishes that make up this menu. It's a mélange of sweet, salty, and spicy flavors inspired by the cooking of both the Middle East and the Mediterranean. Figs, sun-dried tomatoes, fennel, za'atar, feta—the ingredients speak techniques to bring out their delicious characteristics.

Straightforward fresh ingredients, simple techniques, and classic combinations—the recipes here could not be easier. And they'll fill your kitchen with the most tantalizing fragrances.

Piquant

Middle Eastern Mixed Greens

Figs, feta, and fennel are tossed with greens and a honey-sweetened dressing spiced with za'atar in this bold salad. A Middle Eastern seasoning of dried thyme, marjoram, sesame seeds, and sumac, za'atar is used as freely in the Middle East as salt and pepper are in the United States. Crunchy, creamy, chewy—the textures in the salad are as interesting as the flavors. I keep Mission figlets (which are smaller and daintier looking than regular figs) always on hand; they lend sophistication to many dishes.

8   cups mixed greens
1   fennel bulb, cored and very thinly sliced
2   cups variously colored cherry tomatoes, halved
1   cup feta cheese, crumbled
1   cup dried Mission figlets, stemmed
    and thinly sliced

Za'atar-Honey Dressing
½   cup extra virgin olive oil
¼   cup rice vinegar
    Juice of 1 lemon
1   tablespoon honey
1   garlic clove, minced
1   tablespoon za'atar
1   teaspoon dried basil
    Freshly ground black pepper

Place the mixed greens in a large bowl. Top with the fennel followed by the tomatoes and feta. Scatter the fig slices all over. Set aside.

To make the dressing: Combine the olive oil, vinegar, lemon juice, honey, garlic, za'atar, basil, and pepper in a jar with a tight-fitting lid. Shake to thoroughly combine.

Drizzle just enough of the dressing over the salad to lightly coat it; do not soak the greens. Toss until all of the greens are lightly coated. Serve immediately.

Serves 6 to 8

Mediterranean-Style Sea Bass

The assertive flavors of capers, garlic, and sun-dried tomatoes make this 15-minute dish an ideal choice if you're craving the sunny flavors of the Mediterranean. If you want to add a little heat, sprinkle a few crushed red pepper flakes into the food processor before blending the ingredients together.

3   tablespoons capers, drained
8   oil-packed sun-dried tomato slices, plus 3 tablespoons of the oil
4   scallions, white parts only
2   garlic cloves, peeled
    Kosher salt and freshly ground pepper
6   sea bass fillets, about 6 ounces each, skin removed

Combine the capers, sun-dried tomatoes and their oil, the scallions, and garlic in the bowl of a food processor and process until a paste forms, about 1 minute. Season to taste with salt and pepper.

Place the fillets in a single layer in a baking dish. Using the back of a spoon, rub the paste all over the tops of the fillets. The fish can be covered and refrigerated at this point for a few hours.

Preheat the oven to 400°F. Cover the dish with aluminum foil and bake for about 12 minutes, until the fish flakes apart when pricked with a fork.

Serves 6

Lentil Rice with Carrots

→ Image on page 16

An easy-to-prepare dish that is rich in both color and flavor, this is as perfect to serve all year-round as it is light and flavorful. It's the perfect side dish because it goes well with salads, meat, or fish.

2	tablespoons olive oil
3	medium onions, cut into ¼-inch-thick slices
2	carrots, peeled and grated on the medium holes of a box grater
2	cups long-grain white rice
¾	cup dried brown lentils
1	teaspoon kosher salt
½	teaspoon freshly ground black pepper
5	cups boiling water or chicken stock

Preheat the oven to 350°F. Heat the olive oil in a sauté pan over medium heat. Add the onions and sauté until golden, 15 to 20 minutes. Combine ½ cup of the sautéed onions and the carrots in a small bowl and set aside.

Place the rice and lentils in a strainer, rinse under cold running water, and drain. Season with salt and pepper.

Spread the carrot and onion mixture evenly over the bottom of a large casserole dish with a tight-fitting lid (or use 2 layers of aluminum foil to cover the dish). Spread the rice mixture evenly over them and top with the remaining onions. Pour the boiling water or stock over the rice and cover the dish tightly with the lid or foil. Bake for 1 hour or until all the water is absorbed and the lentils are firm yet break when pressed between a spoon and the side of the dish. Serve warm.

Serves 8 to 10

Roasted Peppers with Balsamic Glaze

These gorgeous roasted peppers can be served as a salad course or a side dish. Feel free to prepare them in advance; they can be refrigerated for up to 1 month.

2	red bell peppers
2	yellow bell peppers
2	green bell peppers
¼	cup balsamic vinegar
¼	cup extra virgin olive oil
2	tablespoons sugar
4	garlic cloves, minced

Preheat the broiler. Place the whole peppers in a roasting pan and place 3 inches under the broiler. Broil, turning 2 or 3 times, until blackened all over, about 5 minutes total. Transfer to a resealable plastic bag and seal. Set aside for at least 20 minutes to steam the peppers, which makes the skin easy to peel off.

Meanwhile, prepare the glaze: Combine the vinegar, olive oil, sugar, and garlic in a small saucepan over high heat. Bring to a rapid boil and remove from heat. Set aside.

Working with one pepper at a time, gently peel away the blackened skin and discard. The peppers can be kept whole or you may want to halve them and remove the stem and seeds. Transfer to a 32-ounce glass jar. Pour the glaze over the peppers and cover with a tight-fitting lid. Refrigerate for at least 24 hours or up to 1 month.

To serve, bring the peppers to room temperature or heat in the microwave for 20 seconds to allow the glaze to liquefy, then arrange the peppers on a serving dish and drizzle with any remaining glaze from the jar.

Serves 6 to 8

Piquant

Why is it that when I think about indulging in a favorite food, it always involves a spoon? Perhaps it goes back to the first utensil we are introduced to, or that the dishes that require a spoon are generally the most comforting? Creamy, soothing, cooling, juicy: I do know that if I can eat something with a spoon, it tastes better than anything else. Serve all of the dishes here with a fork and a spoon—to corral juices, serve up spicy chutney, and eat tangy hummus by, yes, the spoonful.

Indulgent

Five-Minute Hummus

Before I began making hummus at home, I found myself tossing containers of prepared varieties into my grocery cart, despite their less-than-bright flavor. After making it from scratch, I've never gone back. The beauty of this recipe is that you can add as much or as little lemon or garlic as you like to make it as tangy as desired. Hummus requires a healthy dose of salt and pepper to flavor it; don't be put off by the amount you will have to use to get it tasting just right. I love to sprinkle on a little za'atar, the Middle Eastern spice blend of dried thyme, marjoram, sesame seeds, and sumac, just before serving.

4 (15.5-ounce) cans chickpeas, drained
1-4 garlic cloves, to taste, peeled
¼ cup extra virgin olive oil, plus more for drizzling
    Juice of 2 lemons, plus more to taste
1 heaping tablespoon tahini
    Kosher salt and freshly ground pepper
    Za'atar (optional)

Rinse the chickpeas in a colander under cold running water. Combine the chickpeas, garlic, olive oil, lemon juice, and tahini in the bowl of a food processor and pulse until thoroughly combined. Gradually add enough water, one tablespoon at a time, through the feed tube while pulsing to create the desired consistency. I prefer mine to be a little chunky. Season generously with salt and pepper. Transfer the mixture to a serving dish or container with a tight fitting lid. To help preserve the hummus in the fridge, drizzle olive oil over the top and sprinkle with za'atar, if using. The hummus will keep, tightly covered, in the refrigerator up to 3 weeks.

Makes 4 cups

Jalapeño Chutney

Eat jalapeños every day. Honestly, when people ask me how I stay in shape, this is the advice I give them. I am no doctor, but I'd swear that the super-hot peppers help me stay healthy. And there's no better way to enjoy them than with this spicy condiment—it is perfect on crispy baguette slices, paired with hummus and crackers, or as a sauce with almost any main course. I usually quadruple the recipe; it'll keep for 2 weeks. Use disposable rubber gloves to stem and seed the jalapeños—they can burn: not only your hands but anything you touch afterward!

¼ cup extra virgin olive oil
    Juice of ½ lemon
¼ pound fresh jalapeños, stemmed, seeded, and cut into small dice
3 garlic cloves, minced
1 tablespoon minced fresh flat-leaf parsley
½ teaspoon kosher salt

Combine the olive oil, lemon juice, jalapeños, garlic, parsley, and salt in a bowl and stir to thoroughly combine. Serve immediately or store, tightly covered in the refrigerator, for up to 2 weeks. Let come to room temperature before serving.

Makes about 1 cup

Jalapeño and Tomato Chutney

I must have a spicy component at every meal; a hint of spice simply makes the meal. This savory condiment is perfect paired with hummus, but great on its own with generous slices of challah for dipping. There are two types of dippers: Some take only the sauce, others go for the whole jalapeño!

2   tablespoons olive oil
¾   pound fresh jalapeños (about 10)
8   garlic cloves, peeled and left whole
1   (6-ounce) can tomato paste
1   teaspoon kosher salt
½   teaspoon freshly ground black pepper

In a medium saucepan, heat the oil over medium-high heat. Carefully slide the jalapeños into the pan, taking care not to let the splattering oil burn you. Cover and cook for 3 minutes. Add the garlic, tomato paste, and ½ cup water and stir to combine. Season with the salt and pepper. Reduce the heat to low and cook, covered, until the jalapeños are soft and the sauce coats the back of a spoon. Remove from the heat and cool to room temperature. To store, transfer to a non-reactive container with a tight-fitting lid and refrigerate up to 2 weeks.

Makes about 2 cups

Crispy Cauliflower with Tomatoes and Dill

It seems like everyone is always searching for new, original ideas for tasty vegetable side dishes. Sometimes I find that the best dishes are invented just by throwing together whatever it is I have in my fridge. That's just what happened with this recipe: I had a head of cauliflower, some cherry tomatoes, and a little fresh dill that just needed a squeeze of lemon juice and, of course, olive oil. Rather than cutting the cauliflower into florets (big pieces that look like little trees), the trick here is to slice it into thin slices with a large knife (almost like shaving it down). Then all the thin slices of cauliflower can soak up the lemon-dill flavor and become perfectly buttery-tasting and crunchy in the oven. The night I first made this, we (our friends were over) literally ate it straight out of the baking dish, without a trace left over! So easy and so, so good.

1   cauliflower head, cored and shaved into
    thin slices (with a large knife)
2   handfuls cherry tomatoes
2   tablespoons chopped fresh dill
    Juice of 1 lemon
3   tablespoons olive oil
1   teaspoon kosher salt
½   teaspoon freshly ground black pepper

Preheat the oven to 375°F. Combine the cauliflower, tomatoes, dill, lemon juice, and olive oil in a 9 x 13-inch baking dish, using your hands to toss everything together. Season with the salt and pepper. Bake, uncovered, for 40 minutes to 1 hour, depending how crunchy you like it!

Serves 6

Spicy Tomato-Cucumber Salad

I'm a sucker for Tabasco sauce...
a not-so-glamorous condiment
that fools my guests every time.
They're always trying to guess
which exotic spice I've added to this
refreshing-but-spicy salad. In addition
to the "secret" Tabasco, the recipe
calls for a few specialty ingredients:
preserved lemons and Israeli pickles
(which are nothing more than
gherkins cured in brine). Both can
be found at Middle Eastern grocers,
kosher supermarkets, and sometimes
in a traditional grocery store.

4   ripe beefsteak tomatoes, cut into small dice
4   Kirby cucumbers, peeled and cut into small dice
½   small yellow onion, cut into small dice
4   Israeli pickles, cut into small dice
¼   cup chopped cilantro
¼   cup chopped fresh flat-leaf parsley
2   tablespoons chopped preserved lemons
    or juice of ½ lemon
3   tablespoons extra virgin olive oil
1   teaspoon Tabasco sauce
½   teaspoon kosher salt
¼   teaspoon freshly ground black pepper

Combine the tomatoes, cucumbers, onions, and
pickles in a medium bowl. Toss to combine. Add the
cilantro, parsley, preserved lemon, olive oil, Tabasco,
salt, and pepper and toss to coat evenly. Serve at
room temperature.

Serves 6 to 8

Balsamic-Marinated Chicken with Olives and Sun-Dried Tomatoes

→ Images on pages 11 & 12

The key to this ridiculously succulent chicken is in the extended marinating. Don't skimp on the 24-hour (48 hours is even better!) soak in vinegar—it will bring raves. Avoid using canned olives if at all possible—those in the olive bars at gourmet supermarkets are far superior.

2 whole chickens, cut into 8 pieces
2 cups Kalamata olives, pitted
¾ cup oil-packed sun-dried tomatoes, plus ¼ cup of their oil
½ cup dry white wine
3 tablespoons balsamic vinegar
1 teaspoon kosher salt
½ teaspoon freshly ground black pepper

Combine the chicken, olives, sun-dried tomatoes and their oil, wine, vinegar, salt, and pepper in a large baking dish. Coat the chicken evenly with the marinade, turning the pieces several times with your hands. Cover tightly with aluminum foil and refrigerate for 24 to 48 hours.

Remove the chicken from the refrigerator and bring to room temperature, about 1 hour.

Preheat the oven to 400°F. Turn the chicken in the marinade to coat once again. Bake, uncovered, moving the chicken pieces around several times to allow for even cooking, for about 1 hour, until cooked through.

Serves 8 to 10

I put together this menu for cooks who love to explore new ingredients and are eager to try new techniques. I love taking risks in my cooking—because when a new tack works, it works well. And when it doesn't, well, I always learn something! Combining white peaches with honey, spicing crispy rice cereal with paprika, or spiking a marinade with tequila—these are the kinds of combinations I love to try.

Cooking outside the box gives you latitude in your cooking; it broadens your repertoire (and your pantry) and, ultimately, it makes you a better cook. What's more, serving up the unexpected is always a delicious moment.

Gutsy

Spinach, Haricots Vert, and Avocado Salad with Crunchy Honey Dressing

Crunchy, salty, sweet, and sharp—this salad has it all! The dressing contributes texture with sunflower and sesame seeds as well as sweetness and tang with honey and cider vinegar. All in all, a unique and delicious concoction.

8   cups baby spinach
      Handful haricots verts, trimmed and
      cut into 1-inch pieces
1   avocado, pitted, peeled, and cut into small cubes
1   white peach, skin on, pitted and cut into
      very thin slices
¼   cup sugar
¼   cup honey
¼   cup vegetable oil
¼   cup cider vinegar
1   teaspoon Dijon mustard
1   garlic clove, minced
¼   cup salted shelled sunflower seeds
2   tablespoons sesame seeds

Place the spinach, haricots verts, avocado, and peach in a large bowl or on a large platter. Combine the sugar, honey, vegetable oil, vinegar, mustard, garlic, sunflower seeds, and sesame seeds in a jar with a tight-fitting lid. Shake to thoroughly combine. Drizzle the dressing over the salad and toss to coat all over.

Serves 6 to 8

Japanese Kani Salad

This crunchy, spicy salad is my take on the ubiquitous kani salads on Japanese restaurant menus. The addition of surimi (imitation crabmeat), not to mention spiced rice cereal, takes a basic salad to the next level. I like to buy frozen surimi, making it easy to pull out and use whenever I need it.

Crunchy Topping
¾   cup crisped rice cereal (such as Rice Krispies)
1   teaspoon paprika
1   tablespoon olive oil

Spicy Mayo
½   cup mayonnaise
1-2 tablespoons Tabasco sauce
1   teaspoon sesame oil
1   teaspoon sugar
½   teaspoon chili powder

Salad
8   frozen surimi (imitation crab) sticks (½ of a 16-ounce package), thawed
2   hothouse cucumbers, unpeeled and julienned
1   avocado, cored, peeled, and thinly sliced

To make the topping: Preheat the oven to 400°F. In a medium bowl, combine the cereal, paprika, and olive oil and stir to coat evenly. Spread in a single layer on a baking sheet and bake for about 5 minutes, until golden and toasted.

Meanwhile, prepare the mayo: In a medium bowl, whisk together the mayonnaise, Tabasco, sesame oil, sugar, and chili powder until thoroughly incorporated.

To make the salad: Roll the crabsticks on a hard surface so that they break up into stringy pieces. Place in a large bowl and add the cucumber. Add the mayo and stir to evenly distribute. Transfer the mixture to a serving platter and top with the spiced cereal. Arrange the avocado around the salad. Serve with more Tabasco sauce, if desired.

Serves 6 to 8

Tequila London Broil with Mango Chutney

London broil, otherwise known as "sliced steak," usually refers to the preparation of flank steak: marinated, grilled, or broiled, and then cut against the grain into thin slices. It is a great way to prepare steak because it cooks quickly and makes perfect sandwiches—if there happens to be any left over. This recipe is one that I often serve to my family at home during the week, but just as often offer up to a large crowd at a weekend dinner party. It's simple but sophisticated.

5 pounds London broil (usually comes in 2 pieces)
½ cup soy sauce
¼ cup tequila
   Juice of 2 limes
5 garlic cloves, minced
3 tablespoons minced cilantro
2 tablespoons brown sugar
¼ teaspoon freshly ground black pepper

Spicy Mango Chutney

3 ripe mangoes, cut into ½-inch pieces,
   or 3 cups frozen mango chunks, thawed
¼ cup sugar
   Juice of 2 limes
¼ cup cider vinegar
1 tablespoon minced fresh ginger
½ jalapeño with seeds, minced
½ teaspoon cumin
1 tablespoon minced cilantro
1 tablespoon minced fresh mint leaves

Place the meat in a large resealable plastic bag. In a medium bowl, whisk together the soy sauce, tequila, lime juice, garlic, cilantro, sugar, and pepper. Pour the marinade over the meat and seal the bag. Marinate in the refrigerator overnight.

To make the chutney: In a small saucepan, combine the mango and sugar and bring to a boil over medium-high heat. Reduce the heat to medium and simmer for 10 minutes. Using a fork, mash the mangoes to a chunky consistency. Stir in the lime juice, vinegar, ginger, jalapeño, and cumin. Cook for 5 minutes more. Remove from the heat and stir in the cilantro and mint. Makes about 2 cups. The chutney may be refrigerated, tightly covered, up to 1 week.

Preheat the oven to 400°F. Heat a large grill pan over medium-high heat until very hot. Remove the meat from the bag, reserving the marinade. Sear the meat on the grill until well browned, about 3 minutes per side. Transfer to a baking dish and pour the marinade over. Bake, uncovered, for 15 minutes for medium rare or 20 minutes for medium. Let the meat rest on a cutting board for about 15 minutes before slicing against the grain into ⅛-inch-thick strips. Serve with the chutney.

Serves 12

Gingered Butternut Squash and Sweet Potatoes

Every time I serve this dish, my guests ask: "What is this?!" The creaminess of the butternut squash and sweet potatoes contrasts beautifully with the sharpness of the ginger to create magical flavors. I like to make this in the morning, turn off the oven, and leave it in there all day long. Your house will smell so good, you'll want to make it again and again. Sometimes I make this a day in advance, cover and refrigerate, then reheat in a low oven until warm.

1   large butternut squash, peeled, seeded, and cut into 2-inch wedges
4   sweet potatoes, peeled and cut into 2-inch wedges
3   yellow onions, peeled and thinly sliced
1   (4-inch) piece ginger, peeled and julienned
5   tablespoons olive oil
1   tablespoon kosher salt
½   tablespoon freshly ground black pepper

Preheat the oven to 400°F. Line a baking sheet with parchment paper.

In a large bowl, combine the squash, sweet potatoes, onions, ginger, olive oil, salt, and pepper. Use your hands to mix everything together until the wedges are evenly coated. Transfer to the prepared baking sheet and arrange in a single layer. Bake, uncovered, for 40 minutes. Reduce the temperature to 300°F and bake for an additional 90 minutes. Reduce the oven temperature to 200°F and bake 1 hour longer. The potatoes and squash should be crisp on the outside and soft on the inside. If you are not serving this dish immediately, keep in the oven, with the oven turned off, until serving.

Serves 8

Of all of the dishes I make, the ones in this chapter are among the most satisfying. Earthy beets warmed with cumin, creamy avocado combined with spicy greens and a soothing curry dressing, and a classic kugel given a major makeover—they are all here and they're all so satisfying. They are also fool-proof, simple to make, and as delightful to prepare as they are to eat.

Delectable

Cumin-Spiced Beet Salad

In addition to the warm heat of cumin, I use crushed red pepper flakes to add a little fire to this colorful salad. The contrast between the sweet beets and hot pepper is addictive. I wear rubber gloves when handling beets to prevent my hands from staining; the ruby red spots can last for days!

4	large beets, stem and roots removed, well scrubbed
	Juice of ½ lemon
2	tablespoons white vinegar
1	tablespoon extra virgin olive oil
2	garlic cloves, pushed through a garlic press
2	teaspoons cumin powder
½	teaspoon crushed red pepper flakes
	Kosher salt and freshly ground black pepper

Place the unpeeled beets in a large pot and fill with enough cold water to cover. Bring the water to a boil, reduce the heat to medium, and simmer, uncovered, until the beets are easily pierced with a fork, about 1 hour. Drain and cool for 10 minutes.

Wearing gloves if you like, peel the skins from the beets (they should come off easily). Slice thinly. (I use a crinkle cutter knife that creates zigzag slices.) In a small bowl, whisk together the lemon juice, vinegar, oil, garlic, cumin, and pepper flakes. Place the beets in a large bowl, pour the dressing over, and toss to coat thoroughly. Season generously with salt and pepper. Serve cold or at room temperature. The salad can be refrigerated, covered tightly, up to 1 week.

Serves 6 to 8

I am a salad enthusiast and couldn't disagree more with those who believe a salad is just, well, a salad. This is my most popular, not least because the dressing has a bit of curry powder in it, just the thing to pique anyone's taste buds. Once you taste this, you will keep a jar of the dressing on hand at all times.

8   cups mixed baby greens
1   avocado, pitted, peeled, and cubed
1   red bell pepper, seeded and diced
1   cup vegetable stick snacks (such as Terra Stix)

Curry Dressing
¾   cup extra virgin olive oil
⅓   cup white vinegar
2   tablespoons honey
½   cup packed brown sugar
2   tablespoons curry powder
2   tablespoons yellow mustard
1   garlic clove, crushed through a garlic press
     Pinch kosher salt

Combine the greens, avocado, red pepper, and vegetables sticks in a large salad bowl.

To make the dressing: Combine all the ingredients in a jar with a tight-fitting lid. Cover tightly and shake to combine. Makes about 2 cups. The dressing will keep, covered tightly and refrigerated, for up to 1 month.

Pour about ¼ cup of the dressing over the salad and gently toss to coat. Serve immediately.

Serves 6 to 8

Zucchini and Noodle Kugel

This kugel is not your grandmother's! For an updated, modern kugel, I fiddled with the classic recipe to create a sophisticated and more lady-like, if you will, version. It may put purists off, but there's never any left when I make it!

3 eggs
¾ cup flour
½ cup olive oil
2 tablespoons peach or apricot preserves
1 tablespoon Worcestershire sauce
1 tablespoon Dijon mustard
1 teaspoon kosher salt
½ teaspoon freshly ground black pepper
3 medium zucchini, grated on the medium holes of a grater and drained in a strainer
1 medium yellow onion, grated on the medium holes of a grater
12 ounces fine egg noodles, cooked according to package directions and drained

Preheat the oven to 375°F. Grease an 11 x 14-inch baking dish with oil.

In a large bowl, whisk together the eggs, flour, oil, preserves, Worcestershire, mustard, salt, and pepper. Add the zucchini, onion, and noodles and stir until thoroughly coated and combined.

Scrape the mixture into the prepared baking dish. Bake, uncovered, for about 1 hour, until crisp and golden. (For individual servings, divide the mixture equally among 12 greased 4-ounce ramekins, place on baking sheets, and bake for about 30 minutes, until crisp and golden.)

Serves 12

Best Brisket

The key to an amazing brisket is a perfect sauce, one that goes easy on the sugar. Too many modern-day kosher recipes call for heaps of it, and it's so, so unnecessary. This is the best brisket I've ever tasted. Almost as great as its amazing flavor is that you can make it a month in advance and freeze it. So convenient! Note that you will need a roasting pan that can be used both on a stovetop and in the oven.

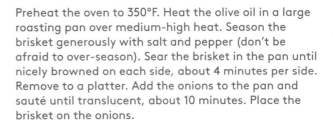

3   tablespoons olive oil
1   (5-pound) first-cut beef brisket
     Kosher salt and freshly ground black pepper
2   medium yellow onions, sliced
1   (12-ounce) bottle beer, such as Corona
¾   cup ketchup
1   (14-ounce) can whole-berry cranberry sauce
¼   cup red wine

Preheat the oven to 350°F. Heat the olive oil in a large roasting pan over medium-high heat. Season the brisket generously with salt and pepper (don't be afraid to over-season). Sear the brisket in the pan until nicely browned on each side, about 4 minutes per side. Remove to a platter. Add the onions to the pan and sauté until translucent, about 10 minutes. Place the brisket on the onions.

In a large bowl, whisk together the beer, ketchup, cranberry sauce, and wine. Pour the mixture over the brisket in the pan and bring to a boil.

Cover the pan with foil and bake in the oven for 1½ hours. Carefully turn the brisket over using tongs. Continue baking, covered, for an additional 1½ hours, until a fork easily pierces the brisket. Using tongs, transfer the brisket to a cutting board.

Place the roasting pan on the stovetop over medium-high heat. Bring the cooking juices to a boil and simmer until the liquid reduces to a thick, velvety sauce, about 10 minutes. Slice the brisket while still warm and serve with the sauce alongside.

The brisket can be made 1 day in advance. To store, let the brisket and sauce cool completely, then wrap the meat in foil and refrigerate. Transfer the sauce to a covered container and refrigerate as well. To serve, slice the brisket when it is cold to prevent it from falling apart. Arrange the slices in a large baking dish and pour the sauce over them. Cover with foil and reheat in a 300°F oven for 40 minutes. The brisket, whole or sliced, and the sauce can also be frozen for up to 4 weeks.

Serves 8 to 10

Flavor always comes first in my recipes. So when I can create a refreshing, new dish from everyday ingredients, nothing makes me happier. But flavor is just one of the important ways to approach food. The colors and shapes of the ingredients can mean the difference between an appetizing plate of food and a bland one.

The menu that follows is a breath of fresh air; the flavor combinations are unusual, as are the colors. Spicy arugula, tart grapefruit, and salty pistachios come together in a beautifully composed salad. Dusky black sesame seeds are a stark contrast to the jewel-toned salmon they coat. The eye is drawn to shards of thinly grated monochromatic celery root floating in a tiny mountain on the plate.

Modern

Winter Arugula Salad with Avocado and Grapefruit

→ Image on page 9

The spiciness of arugula in combination with the saltiness of pistachios and the tang of grapefruit makes this the perfect salad for winter nights. It's filling, refreshing, and comforting all at once—and perfect alongside grilled or roasted meat or fish.

2   bunches (about 5 cups) arugula
1   avocado, pitted, peeled, and thinly sliced
1   grapefruit, peel and pith cut away with a serrated knife and sections cut free from membranes
¼   cup shelled pistachios
⅓   cup good-quality assertively flavored extra virgin olive oil
    Juice of 1 lemon, preferably Meyer
¼   teaspoon kosher salt
½   teaspoon freshly ground black pepper

Combine the arugula, avocado, grapefruit, and pistachios in a large bowl. Pour the olive oil over the salad, followed by the lemon juice. Season with the salt and pepper. Toss to coat and serve immediately.

Serves 6 to 8

Lemony Celery Root Salad with Walnuts

This salad takes me right back to my childhood home in Montreal: It was on the table, without fail, every Friday night. The funny thing is, I hadn't a clue that the primary ingredient was celery root; I just knew that I loved the mild celery-like flavor and creamy texture. I love preparing dishes with somewhat unusual ingredients such as celery root; it's what keeps me interested in cooking.

1   celery root, rough outer skin discarded, root halved
    Juice of 1 lemon
2   tablespoons extra virgin olive oil
¼   cup chopped walnuts, toasted
¼   teaspoon kosher salt
¼   teaspoon freshly ground black pepper

On the large holes of a box grater or in a food processor fitted with the grater disk, grate the celery root. Transfer to a medium serving bowl. Pour the lemon juice and olive oil over the celery root, add the walnuts, and season with the salt and pepper. Toss to thoroughly coat and serve.

Serves 4 to 6

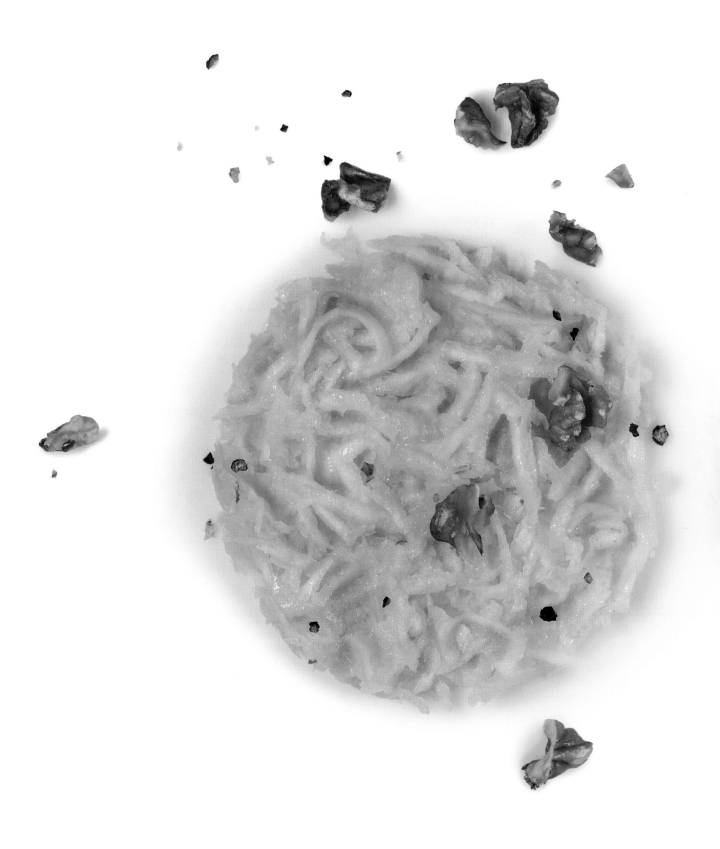

Black Sesame–Crusted Char

Arctic char is a deeply flavorful fish, not unlike trout and salmon. It can range in color from light pink to deep red—vivid jewel tones that perfectly complement the black sesame seed crust. If you can't find Arctic char, use any fish with firm, dense flakes such as salmon, halibut, or trout.

¾   cup soy sauce
½   cup peach preserves, heated
2   tablespoons honey
1   teaspoon ground ginger
1   cup black sesame seeds
1   (2-pound) Arctic char fillet

Combine the soy sauce, preserves, honey, and ginger in a small bowl and whisk until thoroughly combined. Set the marinade aside.

Pour the sesame seeds onto a dinner plate. Heat a large nonstick skillet over high heat. Dip the flesh side of the fillet into the sesame seeds and gently push down until the flesh is completely coated in seeds. Slip the char into the hot pan, seed side down, and sear until the seeds adhere, about 1 minute.

Place the char, skin side down, in a large baking dish and pour the marinade over it. Cover and marinate in the refrigerator for at least 15 minutes or up to 3 hours.

Preheat the oven to 350°F. Bake the char, uncovered, until plump, about 20 minutes. Cover with foil and bake for 10 minutes longer, until the fish flakes apart when pricked with a fork.

To serve, transfer the char to a rectangular serving dish and cut into individual portions using a knife and spatula. Cutting into this gorgeous dish is part of the delight because of the intense colors.

Serves 8

Grilled Eggplant, Sun-Dried Tomato, and Bocconcini Salad

Do it once and you will see the wisdom of grilling sliced eggplant in batches, allowing them to cool completely, and then freezing them in single layers in large freezer bags. When you have them on hand, you can make this salad in just minutes. The combination of flavors in this vibrant salad is delicious and unusual. Bocconcini ("small mouthfuls") are small mozzarella balls packed in water or olive oil; they can be found in most supermarkets.

1   large eggplant, cut into ¼-inch-thick rounds
     Olive oil, for brushing the grill pan
1   cup oil-packed sun-dried tomatoes, plus
     2 tablespoons of their oil
½   cup bocconcini packed in oil
6   fresh basil leaves, torn into small pieces
3   tablespoons balsamic vinegar
     Kosher salt and freshly ground black pepper

Preheat the oven to 350°F. Place the eggplant slices in a colander and sprinkle with salt. Set aside for 10 minutes. Meanwhile, prepare a grill or heat a grill pan over high heat. Brush the pan with olive oil.

Pat the eggplant slices dry and grill until translucent and charred, about 3 minutes per side. Transfer the eggplant to a baking sheet and bake until soft, about 10 minutes. (At this point, the cooked eggplant can be stored in resealable plastic bags and frozen for up to 3 months. To use, thaw at room temperature until softened.)

Place the eggplant slices on a serving plate. Scatter the sun-dried tomatoes over, then drizzle the tomato oil on top. Scatter the bocconcini and basil on top. Drizzle with the balsamic vinegar and season with salt and pepper before serving. The dish can be made a day in advance, covered, and refrigerated. Bring to room temperature before serving.

Serves 6 to 8

My kitchen is the most inspiring room in my home. I suppose it makes sense, as I prefer to spend more time there than in any other part of the house. Whenever I'm in there, I'm inspired—inspired to cook, create, and bring comfort to anyone around me through lovingly prepared food. I love experimenting in the kitchen, trying to come up with a new take on a tired dish, or injecting a little verve into a tried-and-true classic.

But beyond the cooking, I am always thinking about beautiful ways to present a dish. This menu highlights some of the unique flavor combinations I've come up with and it serves as a nice selection for entertaining. When I serve this dinner, the conversation inevitably turns to what's on the plate. What more could a home cook want?

Clever

The classic goat cheese–beet pairing
is delicious on its own, but add pecans
and pomegranate seeds to the mix
and they take this salad to another
dimension! I love using garlic-flavored
goat cheese here—it complements the
beets beautifully.

8   cups mixed baby greens
4   small beets (red and/or golden), boiled, peeled,
     and thinly sliced (see page 98)
¾   cup crumbled goat cheese
½   cup pecans, toasted and coarsely chopped
½   cup pomegranate seeds or dried cherries
¼   cup Curry Dressing (page 100)

Place the greens and beets in a large bowl. Scatter
the goat cheese, pecans, and pomegranate seeds on
top. Drizzle the dressing over the salad and toss to
thoroughly coat the greens. Serve immediately.

Serves 6 to 8

Eggplant Napoleons

→ Image on page 5

Spinach, zucchini, and sun-dried tomatoes make up the layers of these pretty vegetable stacks that are slicked with fresh herb-infused olive oil. The herb oil is also excellent for brushing on any grilled vegetable. In order for the herbs to thoroughly infuse the oil, make it 2 days in advance and refrigerate. It will keep for up to 3 weeks.

Herb Oil
1   cup extra virgin olive oil
     Splash balsamic vinegar
2   garlic cloves, pushed through a garlic press
½   cup mixed fresh herbs, such as basil, thyme, and rosemary

Napoleons
     Olive oil, for brushing the grill pan
1   large eggplant, sliced into ¼-inch-thick rounds
     Kosher salt
1   zucchini, sliced into ½-inch-thick rounds, brushed with olive oil
1   tablespoon extra virgin olive oil
1   shallot, minced
1   (10-ounce) package frozen chopped spinach, thawed and squeezed of liquid
½   teaspoon cumin
     Freshly ground black pepper
8   oil-packed sun-dried tomatoes, cut into quarters
     Fresh basil leaves, for garnish

To make the herb oil: Combine the olive oil, vinegar, garlic, and herbs in a jar or squeeze bottle. Refrigerate for at least 2 days or up to 3 weeks.

To make the napoleons: Preheat the oven to 350°F and prepare a grill over high heat. Arrange the eggplant slices in a colander and sprinkle with salt. Set aside for 10 minutes.

Brush the grill with olive oil. Pat the eggplant dry and grill, turning once, for about 3 minutes per side, until nice char marks appear. Drizzle with a bit of herb oil and arrange on a baking sheet. Bake for about 10 minutes, until soft. Set aside.

Meanwhile, grill the zucchini, turning once, for about 2 minutes per side, until char marks form.

Arrange on a second baking sheet, drizzle with some herb oil, and bake for 10 minutes, until soft.

Heat the olive oil in a sauté pan over medium-high heat. Add the shallot and cook until lightly browned. Stir in the spinach and cumin and sauté until it appears dry, about 4 minutes. Season with salt and pepper.

To assemble the napoleons, place an eggplant round on a plate, top with a zucchini slice followed by another eggplant slice, a teaspoon of spinach, and another eggplant slice. Top with a few pieces of sun-dried tomato. Repeat to make about 10 napoleons. They can be prepared up to this point several hours in advance and kept at room temperature. Just before serving, drizzle with a little herb oil and garnish with fresh basil.

Serves 6 to 8

Marinated Vegetable Salad

The longer this salad marinates, the more flavorful it is. It's my go-to summer Sunday night salad; I make enough to last for the week!

1   pound haricots verts, trimmed
4   carrots, peeled and cut into thin julienne
2   cups sugar snap peas, trimmed
1   cup frozen shelled edamame, thawed
1   large bunch asparagus, trimmed and cut into 2-inch pieces
½   small red onion, very thinly sliced
3   tablespoons minced fresh ginger
½   cup rice vinegar
2   tablespoons toasted sesame oil
1   teaspoon kosher salt
½   teaspoon freshly ground black pepper

Combine the haricots verts, carrots, snap peas, edamame, asparagus, onion, ginger, rice vinegar, sesame oil, salt, and pepper in a gallon-size resealable bag or a rigid container and seal. Marinate in the refrigerator for 1 hour or up to 1 week. Bring to room temperature before serving.

Serves 8 to 10

Clever

Salmon en Croute

This is the ultimate company dish,
not only because it is so delicious but
because the presentation will give
the impression that you spent hours
and hours cooking the meal. A side
of salmon, along with miso-flavored
mushrooms and spinach, is enclosed
in a golden cloak of puff pastry.

1 sheet puff pastry (½ of a 17-ounce package)
1 tablespoon olive oil
1 (10-ounce) package frozen chopped spinach, thawed and squeezed of liquid
2 cups sliced mixed mushrooms (shiitake, maitake, oyster, or portobello)
3 tablespoons mirin
2 tablespoons white miso
1 tablespoon brown sugar
1 side salmon, about 1½ pounds, skin removed
1 egg, beaten

Miso Sauce
3 tablespoons mirin
3 tablespoons white miso
3 tablespoons brown sugar

Preheat the oven to 400°F.

On a piece of parchment paper, roll out the puff pastry 1 to 2 inches longer than the length and more than twice the width of the salmon fillet. Slide the pastry and paper onto a baking sheet, cover, and refrigerate.

Heat the oil in a sauté pan over high heat. Add the spinach and mushrooms and quickly sauté until the mushrooms are a little browned and the spinach has shrunk a bit in size. Whisk together the mirin, miso, and brown sugar and stir into the spinach and mushrooms. Remove from the heat and let cool.

Place the fish fillet on the dough rectangle, positioning it 3 inches in from one edge. Spread the spinach mixture evenly over the fish. Fold the dough over the fish (like a book) and tuck the top edges under the bottom edges, using your fingertips to seal the dough and making sure the seam is on the underside of the packet. Use a sharp knife to make about 10 slits in the top of the pastry. Brush the top with the beaten egg. Bake until the pastry is golden brown, about 40 minutes. To check the doneness, carefully turn the pastry over and cut a slit into the underside to peek in and check that the fish is done. If it isn't, return to the oven for a few minutes.

Meanwhile, prepare the miso sauce: Whisk together the mirin, miso, and brown sugar until well blended. Keep at room temperature or warm on the stovetop before serving.

To serve, cut the salmon crosswise into 8 to 10 slices, drizzle each with the miso sauce, and serve.

Serves 8 to 10

Master the simple sauces and dressings in the recipes that follow and you will have a lifetime of options for brightening almost any kind of protein, grain, or salad. In my opinion, a great sauce can make or break a dish; the key is to taste as you go and season just so. Over time, whipping up a miso or curry dressing will become rote—you won't even need a recipe.

The beauty of the sauces here is that they are chameleons; they can be used interchangeably depending on your whim. Use the combinations here as a starting point, then take them in any direction you like. And know that in the end, drizzled over just about anything, these sauces make for perfect bitefuls every time.

Saucy

Heirloom Tomatoes with Mint and Cilantro

A splash of white wine not only brightens this salad but gives it a whiff of sophistication. You can use whatever soft herbs you have on hand, but the mint and cilantro combination is among my favorites and a nice departure from the classic tomato-basil pairing.

6 heirloom tomatoes in a variety of shapes and colors, cut into ½-inch-thick slices
3 tablespoons chopped fresh mint leaves
3 tablespoons chopped cilantro
2 tablespoons minced red onion
1 avocado, pitted, peeled, and cut into small cubes
3 tablespoons extra virgin olive oil
   Juice of ½ lemon
   Splash white wine
¼ teaspoon kosher salt
¼ teaspoon freshly ground black pepper

Place the tomatoes and their juices in a serving bowl or on a serving tray. Scatter the mint, cilantro, and red onion over the tomatoes followed by the avocado. Drizzle the olive oil over, followed by the lemon juice and white wine. Season with the salt and pepper and toss well.

Serves 6 to 8

Storing Fresh Herbs

I like to clean my fresh herbs as soon as I bring them home from the supermarket. A salad spinner makes the job quick and easy: First, fill a bowl with cold water. Plunge the herbs into it and gently move with your fingers to release any trapped dirt or grit. Lift the herbs out of the water and transfer to a colander to drain. Line the basket of a salad spinner with a paper towel. Place the herbs in the spinner and spin until completely dry. Wrap the clean herbs in fresh paper towel and store in a resealable bag. The herbs will keep for up to 1 week.

Crab and Mango Salad in Wonton Cups

→ Image on page 7

These little pastries make a wonderful appetizer and are a fun and easy way to serve your favorite bite-sized salad. The cups, wonton wrappers baked in mini muffin tins, can be prepared up to 3 days in advance, thoroughly cooled, and stored in an air-tight container.

24 frozen wonton wrappers, thawed
8 frozen surimi (imitation crabmeat) sticks (½ of a 16-ounce package)
1 hothouse cucumber, peeled and thinly julienned (optional)
1 mango, peeled and cut into small cubes
3 tablespoons chopped cilantro
Crushed red hot pepper flakes (optional)

Miso Dressing
2 tablespoons white miso
2 tablespoons rice vinegar
1 tablespoon mirin
1 tablespoon soy sauce
1 tablespoon light brown sugar

Preheat the oven to 375°F. Coat the cups of a mini muffin tin with nonstick cooking spray. Place one wonton wrapper into each muffin mold, forming small cups. Bake for 8 to 10 minutes, watching them closely as they burn quickly, until golden brown.

String the surimi as you would string cheese and place in a large bowl. Add the cucumber (if using), mango, and cilantro and toss.

To make the miso dressing: Combine the miso, vinegar, mirin, soy sauce, and brown sugar in a jar with a tight-fitting lid and shake to thoroughly combine.

Dress the salad with the dressing, one spoonful at a time and tossing as you go, until the ingredients are thoroughly coated. Divide the salad equally among the wonton cups just before serving. Garnish with red pepper flakes, if desired.

Makes 24 salad cups

Curried Couscous Salad

At first, my mother, who hails from Morocco, did not approve of my version of her country's staple, but everyone who tries this couscous salad—including, eventually, her—seems to love it! It is an unfailing crowd-pleaser, and so easy to prepare. It also keeps well and, in fact, tastes better days after it is made.

1½   cups couscous
1   tablespoon butter or margarine
1½   cups boiling water
4   scallions, minced
¼   cup pine nuts, toasted
¼   cup dried cherries
3   tablespoons chopped cilantro

Curry Dressing
½   cup rice vinegar
⅓   cup extra virgin olive oil
3   tablespoons sugar
1   tablespoon curry powder
½   teaspoon turmeric
         Kosher salt and freshly ground black pepper

Put the couscous in a large bowl. Place the butter in a small bowl and pour the boiling water over it. Stir until the butter is melted, then pour over the couscous. Stir once. Cover with plastic wrap and set aside for 15 minutes.

Meanwhile, prepare the dressing: Combine the vinegar, olive oil, sugar, curry powder, and turmeric in a jar with a tight-fitting lid. Shake to thoroughly combine. Season with salt and pepper.

Fluff the couscous with a fork, breaking all the little clumps apart. Stir in the scallions, pine nuts, cherries, and cilantro. Pour the dressing over and mix well. The salad will keep, covered tightly, in the refrigerator up to 1 week.

Serves 8

Sticky Beef Ribs

These are meant to be eaten with your hands, so offer up lots of napkins for dabbing fingers slicked with the sweet sauce! I typically use a large disposable roasting pan here; it makes cleanup a snap.

5   pounds beef spare ribs
½   cup honey
½   cup ketchup or tomato paste
½   cup soy sauce
¼   cup olive oil
3   garlic cloves, minced
2   tablespoons dried rosemary

Place the ribs in a large roasting pan. Combine the honey, ketchup, soy sauce, olive oil, garlic, and rosemary in a small bowl and pour over the ribs. Cover tightly with foil and marinate in the refrigerator overnight.

Preheat the oven to 400°F. Bake the ribs, covered, for 30 minutes. Reduce the temperature to 350°F and bake for 2 hours more, until the ribs are sticky on the outside and soft on the inside. The ribs can be made in advance and frozen in the marinade for up to 1 month, or refrigerated overnight and reheated in a 300°F oven the next day.

Serves 4 to 6

Sesame Vegetables

I came up with this recipe when I was thinking about how I could make sesame noodles in a healthier way: How about using string beans, haricots verts, or yellow waxed beans instead of noodles? I like to halve the beans lengthwise to make them look even more like noodles. The salad will keep, covered tightly, in the refrigerator up to 1 week.

1 pound haricots verts, trimmed
¼ cup soy sauce
¼ cup rice vinegar
1 heaping tablespoon smooth peanut butter
1 heaping teaspoon tahini
1 teaspoon toasted sesame oil
1 tablespoon grated fresh ginger
1 garlic clove, minced
¼ cup toasted sesame seeds
1 teaspoon crushed red pepper flakes
2 tablespoons freshly snipped chives

Bring a large pot of generously salted water to a rapid boil. Add the haricots verts and cook until bright green, about 3 minutes. Transfer to a colander to drain and rinse under cold water. In a small bowl, whisk together the soy sauce, vinegar, peanut butter, tahini, sesame oil, ginger, and garlic. Pour over the haricots verts and let sit for 20 minutes. Garnish with the sesame seeds, pepper flakes, and chives and serve.

Serves 6

What's a wonderful meal without dessert? When it comes to the sweet moment in the meal, I think less is more. When you use fresh, top-quality ingredients, a few bitefuls is all it really takes to satisfy even the most assertive sweet tooth. Fresh fruits, gourmet chocolate, fragrant spices, fresh butter, and egg—the better the ingredients, the more satisfying the results.

Sweet

My friend Sharone introduced me to
this exotic fruit salad. It's so refreshing
and a nice departure from typical
summer fruit salads.

4   (1-pound) cans lychees in syrup, drained,
     1 cup syrup reserved
¼   watermelon, seeded and cut into chunks
1   pint raspberries
3   tablespoons roughly chopped fresh mint leaves
     Honey, for drizzling
½   cup shelled pistachios, lightly toasted
     and chopped

In a large bowl, combine the lychees and their syrup
with the melon and raspberries. Gently stir in the mint
leaves. Spoon into individual bowls, drizzle with honey,
and sprinkle pistachios over the tops.

Serves 6 to 10

Cinnamon-Hazelnut Pavlova with Raspberries

Nigella Lawson, one of my absolute favorite celeb chefs, got me hooked on her pavlova. I made it so many times that I began to adapt it as I went along. The recipe below is a reflection of all this toying around. The dessert is like a work of art and has all the essentials a great dessert should have: the glossy meringue shell is crisp and rich, the whipped cream topping is soft and delectable, and the raspberries add the perfect dose of tartness. Once you get the hang of making these, it's pure joy.

6	large egg whites
2	cups granulated sugar
¼	cup skinned hazelnuts, ground
1	tablespoon cinnamon
1	teaspoon balsamic vinegar
2	cups heavy cream
½	cup packed dark brown sugar
	Pinch of kosher salt
4	cups raspberries

Preheat the oven to 350°F. Line a baking sheet with parchment paper.

In a large bowl of an electric mixer fitted with the whisk attachment, beat the egg whites on medium speed until satiny peaks form. Add the granulated sugar, ¼ cup at a time, and continue beating until the meringue becomes stiff and very shiny. Using a spatula, fold in the hazelnuts, cinnamon, and balsamic vinegar.

Spoon the meringue onto the prepared baking sheet, forming a 10-inch circle that is about 2 inches thick. Place in the oven, and immediately turn the temperature down to 300°F. Bake for about 1 hour and 15 minutes, until the meringue looks and feels dry. Let cool in a dry place overnight.

Invert the pavlova onto a serving dish, peel away the parchment, and flip over onto the dish. Combine the cream and brown sugar in a large bowl of an electric mixer fitted with the whisk attachment. Whisk on medium speed until soft peaks form. Spoon the whipped cream into the center of the pavlova, leaving a 1-inch border. Sprinkle the raspberries over the whipped cream and serve.

Serves 10

La Pasta (Orange Sponge Cake)

Cake in Spanish is *pastel*. Many Spanish-speaking Jews who came from Morocco would make this simple, light cake to serve on the Sabbath and referred to it as pasta, a twist on *pastel*. The syrup and candied orange slices can be made one day in advance, covered separately, and refrigerated. Return the orange slices to room temperature and rewarm the syrup slightly before serving.

6	large eggs
1¾	cups sugar
½	cup rice bran oil or vegetable oil
½	cup orange juice
1	teaspoon vanilla
2	cups all-purpose flour, sifted
2	teaspoons baking powder

Candied Orange Slices and Syrup

1	cup sugar
¾	cup orange blossom honey
3	tablespoons green cardamom pods, crushed
1	teaspoon vanilla
1	small orange, peel on, thinly sliced

Preheat the oven to 325°F. Grease a 9-inch Bundt pan with oil.

Using a standing or handheld mixer fitted with the whisk attachment, beat the eggs and sugar on medium-high speed until pale yellow and smooth, about 4 minutes. Add the oil, orange juice, and vanilla and beat until thoroughly combined. Add the flour, 1 cup at a time, and baking powder, until thoroughly incorporated. Pour the batter into the prepared pan and bake for about 1 hour, until the cake springs back when tapped or a cake tester inserted into the cake comes out clean. Let cool.

Meanwhile, prepare the candied orange slices: Line a baking sheet with parchment paper. Bring the sugar, honey, cardamom, and 3 cups of water to a boil in a medium-heavy saucepan, stirring until the sugar dissolves. Stir in the vanilla and add the orange slices. Reduce the heat to medium-low and simmer, turning the orange slices occasionally, until they are tender and the syrup is reduced to 3¼ cups, about 40 minutes. Arrange the orange slices in a single layer on the baking sheet. Strain the syrup and reserve.

Remove the cooled cake from the pan and place on a cake platter. Drizzle the syrup over the top of the cake and arrange the orange slices on top. The cake may be covered tightly in plastic wrap 2 days in advance of serving.

Makes one 9-inch cake, serving 8 to 10

Medjool Dates Stuffed with Walnuts

→ Image on page 3

I love a dessert that takes 5 minutes to prepare—not only is this one remarkably simple but it's a reminder how delicious food can be in its natural state. Like a little gift, the sweet dates are "unwrapped" to uncover a savory walnut. Perfection. Without trying too hard.

12 Medjool dates
12 walnut halves
    Good-quality honey

Use a sharp knife to cut a small slit into the top of each date, gently squeeze out the pit, and discard. Push the walnut into the opening, and seal using your fingertips. Repeat with the remaining dates and walnuts. Drizzle very lightly with honey and serve.

Serves 6

Vanilla Sugar

2 cups granulated sugar
1 whole fresh vanilla bean, split

Put the sugar in an airtight container. Scrape the seeds into the container, then tuck the bean into the sugar and seal tightly. Let sit for 1 to 2 weeks. The sugar can be used in any instance granulated sugar is called for in a recipe.

Rustic Apple Tart

→ Image on page 18

Store-bought puff pastry dough is a wonderful time-saver that can help you easily create wonderful pastries and desserts. This sexy, crisp apple tart is the proof. It has become a staple in my home and the home of all my friends. It takes just a few minutes to prepare, uses ingredients you most probably have on hand, and is truly beautiful and delicious.

2 sheets puff pastry (one 17-ounce package), Slightly thawed
3 granny Smith apples, peeled, cored, and quartered
¼ cup granulated sugar
2 tablespoons Vanilla Sugar, page 140
1 teaspoon cinnamon
2 tablespoons unsalted butter, cut into tiny pieces
1 egg, beaten
¼ cup apricot or peach jam, melted

Preheat the oven to 400°F. On a piece of parchment paper, roll out one of the pastry sheets until it is about 14 x 9 inches. Transfer to a baking sheet. From the second sheet of pastry, cut enough 1½-inch-wide strips to form a border around the rolled-out pastry sheet. Brush the rim of the large rectangle lightly with water. Arrange the strips around the rim of the pastry sheet to form a border. Cover and refrigerate.

Using a sharp knife, make a series of slits in the apple quarters along the peeled sides, taking care not to slice all the way through. Place the apples in a microwave-safe bowl, add 2 tablespoons water, and cover with plastic wrap. Microwave for 3 minutes; drain. Combine the sugars and the cinnamon in a small bowl. Sprinkle half of the mixture over the center of the pastry shell. Place the apples over the sugar, slit sides up. Sprinkle the remaining sugar over apples and scatter the butter pieces all over. Brush the rim of the tart with the beaten egg.

Bake the tart until nicely browned, about 25 minutes. If the rim browns before the apples are cooked through, cover it with foil. Brush the jam over the apples and rim and serve warm.

Serves 10 to 12

Cinnamon Sand Cookies

→ Image on page 21

I call these "sand cookies" because of their soft yet grainy, melt-in-your-mouth texture. They're so simple and buttery, the perfect pairing with a hot cup of coffee. And here's a terrific bonus: the delectable little gems can be made dairy-free. One recipe yields about 50 small cookies, which can be stored in the fridge for up to 2 months. Using a mini ice-cream scooper makes the job of rolling the cookies a lot easier, and the consistent size helps to insure they'll bake evenly.

1   cup (2 sticks) unsalted butter or margarine, slightly softened
¾   cups rice bran oil or vegetable oil
1   teaspoon vanilla
1   cup sugar
½   cup finely ground almonds, pecans, or walnuts—it's your choice
½   teaspoon baking powder
1   teaspoon plus 2 tablespoons cinnamon
3-4 cups all-purpose flour

Preheat the oven to 350°F. Line 3 baking sheets with parchment paper.

In the bowl of an electric mixer fitted with the paddle attachment, beat the butter, oil, vanilla, sugar, nuts, baking powder, and the 1 teaspoon cinnamon on high speed until well combined, about 2 minutes. Add ⅓ cup water and mix on low speed. Add the flour, ½ a cup at a time, until a dough is formed. The dough should be smooth and soft, but only a tiny bit sticky. The key is that you should easily be able to roll it into small balls without it sticking to your fingers.

Use a mini ice-cream scooper to scoop out tablespoon-sized portions of the dough. For each portion, use your hands to roll it into a ball and gently press down on the top with your fingertips. Place the cookies on the baking sheets, about 1 inch apart.

Fill a small plastic bag (such as a Ziploc snack bag) with the 2 tablespoons cinnamon. Snip a teensy-tiny hole in the corner of the bag to allow a tiny bit of the cinnamon to pour out. Get a good grip on and good control of the cinnamon bag by twisting it tight, then dab a dot of cinnamon into the center of each cookie.

Bake the cookies, one sheet at a time, for about 25 minutes, until slightly golden. Cool and store in an airtight container in the refrigerator until they are all eaten up!

Makes 50 cookies

Halvah, a crumbly confection made from sesame paste, is one of those foods you either love or hate. I am squarely in the former camp. It is a wonderful ingredient to work with because it is easy to mold and crumble and I find that its exoticism always draws attention. This is a great make-ahead dessert, perfect for having on hand in the freezer for a first-rate, last-minute treat. Look for halvah—plain and flavored with a variety of chocolate and nuts—in specialty food stores. Mini pannetone molds can be found in specialty baking supply stores and at Amazon.com.

1   **pound halvah, variety of your choice**
1   **(16-ounce) container sorbet, such as coconut**
1   **(16-ounce) container gelato, such as hazelnut**
4   **ounces good-quality milk or dark chocolate**

Place 8 paper mini pannetone molds on a baking sheet.

Place the halvah in a large bowl and use a fork to mash into tiny pieces. Divide equally among the 8 molds, using your fingertips to press it into the bottom and smoothing the top.

Meanwhile, allow the sorbet to soften on the counter for about 5 minutes. Divide the sorbet equally among the 8 molds, about 3 tablespoons each, and use the back of a spoon to press it over the halvah and smooth the top. Freeze for about 2 hours, until very firm.

Once the sorbet layer is frozen, repeat the process with the gelato. Freeze the towers overnight.

Peel away the paper molds, cover tightly in plastic wrap, and return to the freezer until ready to serve. Using a vegetable peeler, shave the chocolate into thin shavings. Sprinkle each tower generously with the chocolate shavings and serve.

Serves 8

Plum Crumb Cake with Star Anise

This wonderfully simple plum cake recipe was given to me by a good friend. Wanting to spice it up a bit, I added star anise for its mysterious licorice flavor. I love experimenting with unusual flavors and like to think that the star anise adds a bit of sophistication. That said, the cake can surely be made without the star anise, and the plums can simply be replaced with any fresh stone fruit, such as peaches or apricots.

10 tablespoons (1¼ sticks) unsalted butter
⅔ cup granulated sugar
4 large egg yolks
2 teaspoons vanilla
1¼ cups all-purpose flour
1 teaspoon baking powder
3 cups quartered pitted plums, unpeeled (about 1¼ pounds)

Topping

6 tablespoons (¾ stick) unsalted butter
⅔ cup packed light brown sugar
1 cup all-purpose flour
¼ cup rolled oats
Pinch star anise powder
1 whole star anise
Confectioners' sugar, for garnish

Preheat the oven to 350°F. Grease a 10-inch round springform pan with oil and line the bottom with a round of parchment paper.

To prepare the cake: In the bowl of a standing mixer fitted with the paddle attachment, combine the butter and granulated sugar until creamy. Add the yolks, one at a time, and beat until incorporated, then add the vanilla. Sift in the flour and baking powder and stir until combined. Spread the batter into the prepared pan. It may seem like there isn't enough to go around, but use wet hands to spread the batter over the bottom of the pan. Arrange the plums, skin side down, over the batter, leaving a 1-inch space between the edge and the plums.

To prepare the topping: In the bowl of a standing mixer fitted with a paddle attachment, combine the butter and brown sugar and beat until soft. Add the flour, rolled oats, and star anise powder. Using your fingertips, rub the butter mixture into the dry ingredients until the mixture begins to clump together. Sprinkle the topping over the top of the cake. Place the whole star anise in the center of the cake, pushing down slightly to secure it in the crumb topping. Bake the cake for about 50 minutes, until golden brown. Let cool completely.

Unmold the cake, peel away the parchment paper, and place on a serving plate. Tap some confectioners' sugar through a sieve onto the top of the cake for decoration.

Makes one 10-inch cake, serving 12

Broken Dark Chocolate Cake

→ Image on page 21

The imperfection of this cake is what makes it taste so perfect. A crackled, broken dark top reveals its chocolate density in a unique and beautiful way. When you cut into it, you see various textures: smooth intense chocolate contrasts with a crumbly, light, and flaky shell. Just a reminder that a dessert need not be fancy or decorative to be beautiful.

12	ounces fine-quality dark chocolate (not unsweetened), chopped
¾	cup (1½ sticks) unsalted butter, cut into pieces plus more for the pan
1	vanilla bean, split
¼	teaspoon sea salt
1¼	cups sugar
5	large eggs, separated
¼	cup all-purpose flour

Preheat the oven to 350°F. Grease a 9-inch springform pan with butter, and line the bottom with a round of parchment paper.

Place the chocolate and butter in a large glass or metal bowl. Set the bowl over a pan of water that has just been boiled. Whisk the chocolate and butter together as they melt over the hot water. Use the tip of a sharp knife to scrape the seeds out of the vanilla pod into the chocolate and continue whisking. Whisk in the salt and ½ cup of the sugar. Add the yolks one at a time, whisking well after each addition. Whisk in the flour.

In a large bowl of an electric mixer fitted with the whisk attachment, beat the egg whites with a pinch of salt on high speed until they are soft. Add the remaining ¾ cup sugar, one tablespoon at a time, and continue to beat until the whites hold stiff glossy peaks.

Whisk about 1 cup of the egg whites into the chocolate mixture to lighten, then fold in the remaining whites gently but thoroughly. Pour the batter into the prepared pan and spread evenly. Bake for 40 minutes, until top appears crackled and firm.

Cool the cake completely. Remove the cake from the pan, inverting it onto a large plate. Carefully remove the bottom of the springform pan and peel off the parchment paper. Invert the cake onto a plate and serve. The cake can be made 2 days in advance and wrapped in plastic wrap.

Makes one 9-inch cake, serving 12

Chocolate Chiffon Cake

→ Image on page 19

This recipe comes from my cousin Kelly who lives in Melbourne, Australia. She's told me that it's an old recipe that has gone around her community and that everyone bakes it. She made it for me when I visited, and I immediately fell in love. Unlike the density of the Broken Dark-Chocolate Cake, this cake is light and fluffy and stands incredibly tall.

It's not only a gorgeous cake, it makes a perfect birthday cake. You will need a proper nonstick angel food cake pan for this recipe; it's available at all kitchen and baking supplies stores.

1½ cups all-purpose flour
1½ cups sugar
1½ cups good-quality hot chocolate mix (I like to use Ghiradelli or another premium brand; feel free to use plain chocolate flavor, or add mocha, hazelnut, or any other flavor)
¾ cup rice bran oil or vegetable oil
7 large eggs, separated
2 teaspoons baking powder
1 teaspoon vanilla
   Old-fashioned chocolate syrup (I use Hershey's), for drizzling

Preheat the oven to 350°F. In a large bowl of an electric mixer fitted with the paddle attachment, combine the flour, 1 cup of the sugar, the chocolate mix, oil, egg yolks, baking powder, vanilla, and ¾ cup water. Beat on high speed for 7 minutes until the color becomes a shade or two paler than you started with.

In a separate large bowl with the electric mixer, beat the egg whites and the remaining ½ cup sugar on high until stiff, glossy peaks form. Slowly fold the chocolate mixture into the egg whites using a spatula until both mixtures are well incorporated.

Pour the batter into an ungreased nonstick angel food cake pan. Bake for 1 hour and 15 minutes. You will know the cake is ready when the top has a slight glisten to it. You may also shake the pan ever so slightly to be sure the cake is cooked through (it should not be at all wobbly in the middle). Immediately invert the cake in its pan onto the counter and let cool completely. Once the cake is cooled completely, carefully remove it from the pan by Inverting it one more time onto a cake plate or platter. Drizzle lots and lots of old-fashioned chocolate syrup over the top.

Makes one 10-inch cake, serving 12

Fig and Pecan Biscotti

These no-frills biscotti are perfect with a cup of tea or served with sorbet for a sweet ending to a dinner party. I tore the recipe out of an Australian cooking magazine while traveling through the country five years ago and have turned to it again and again when I want to make something simple, sweet, and beautiful.

⅓ cup sugar
3 large eggs
1¼ cups all-purpose flour
¾ cup pecans
½ cup mission figlets, stemmed

Preheat the oven to 350°F. Line a loaf pan with parchment paper with excess paper overhanging the 2 long edges. In a bowl of an electric mixer fitted with the whisk attachment, whisk together the sugar and eggs until pale yellow and smooth, about 4 minutes. Using a wooden spoon, stir in the flour, pecans, and figlets. Don't overmix.
Pour the mixture into the prepared pan. Bring the sides of the parchment paper together and fold over to tighten so the loaf takes on a more rounded shape. Bake for 45 minutes, until golden and cooked through. Cool completely, wrap in foil, and refrigerate overnight.

Preheat the oven to 300°F. Line a baking sheet with parchment paper. Using a very sharp knife, cut the log into slices as thin as possible. Place the slices, cut side down, on a baking sheet. Bake for about 20 minutes, until golden.

Makes about 30 biscotti

Crunchy Biscotti with Chocolate, Pecans, and Coconut

My friends go crazy for these, an adaptation of a recipe from *Panache*, a wonderful kosher cookbook created as a fundraiser for Montreal's Jewish General Hospital and edited by Shawna Goodman-Sone. Every time anyone bites into one, they are baffled by an elusive ingredient that makes it so special.

¾ cup olive oil
½ cup sugar
2 large eggs
1 teaspoon vanilla
2 cups all-purpose flour
2 teaspoons baking powder
  Pinch kosher salt
1 cup nutlike nugget cereal, such as Grape Nuts (AKA "the secret ingredient")
¾ cup mini chocolate chips
½ cup toasted pecans (or any type of nuts)
¼ cup grated sweetened coconut

Preheat the oven to 350°F. Line 2 cookie sheets with parchment paper.

In a bowl of an electric mixer fitted with the whisk attachment, whisk together the oil, sugar, eggs, and vanilla until thoroughly combined, about 3 minutes. Using a wooden spoon, stir in the flour, baking powder, and salt, and then the cereal, chocolate chips, nuts, and coconut until evenly combined. Using wet hands, divide the mixture equally into 4 portions. Shape each portion into a 7 x 3-inch log.

Place two logs on each baking sheet. Bake for about 30 minutes, until golden. Let cool 20 minutes. Reduce the oven temperature to 300°F. Using a sharp knife, cut the biscotti into 1-inch-thick slices. Place, cut sides down, on a clean baking sheet and bake for 20 minutes, until golden.

Makes about 30 biscotti

Index

Acknowledgements

Thank you Jon, Milan, Emanuel and Rafaela, for bringing me the greatest joy in my life. Mom, thank you for teaching me to find happiness and pride in everything that I do, especially cooking. Andrew Zuckerman, I thank you for this gift- you are a tremendous talent, and a most generous friend. To all of those who made this book possible: Ilan Greenfield, Nick Lee, Justin Cohen, Tom Crabtree, Kathleen Hackett, James Dunlinson, Alistair Turnbull, Deri Reed ,Victoria Granof, Victor Cohen, Erika Yorio, and Gabrielle Mazaud, a big thank you. To my friends, and my students, you are the ones who pushed me to write this book. Your constant support and enthusiasm are a blessing. And of course the Pekofsky and Kushner families, thank you for all your love and encouragement.